# BRIDGE STORIES

# BRIDGE STORIES
## EVERY BRIDGE HAS A STORY

## THOMAS LEECH

WORD ASSOCIATION PUBLISHERS
www.wordassociation.com
1.800.827.7903

ISBN: 978-1-63385-348-5

Library of Congress Control Number: 2020900552

*Designed and published by*
Word Association Publishers
205 Fifth Avenue
Tarentum, Pennsylvania 15084

www.wordassociation.com
1.800.827.7903

Woodrige Publications, LLC
www.woodridgebooksandmusic.com

# Preface

This book is dedicated to those that love to look at and simply admire the wonder of a bridge.

This book tells a unique story of bridges – bridges from the past, bridges that are the present, bridges from Western Pennsylvania, bridges throughout the US and bridges throughout the world - for every bridge has a story.

This book is a collection of essays and articles that have been written over the past 20 years, initially published by the author in some form in the *Pittsburgh Engineer, Summer Edition*, the official magazine of the *Engineers' Society of Western Pennsylvania*. The Society was founded in 1880 and is the second oldest engineering society in America, predated only the Boston Society of Civil Engineers. Earliest members of the Society included Andrew Carnegie (iron and steel magnate), John Brashaer (millwright, lensmaker & astronomer), and Gustav Lindenthal (eminent bridge designer). Since its founding, the *Engineers' Society of Western Pennsylvania* has continued its tradition of pursuing an educational and scientific mandate. This is best typified by its sponsorship of the International Bridge Conference®, an annual bridge conference attracting engineers and other interested bridge enthusiasts from around the world. As guest editor of the *Pittsburgh Engineer, Summer Edition*, the author has been involved in the planning, soliciting interest for contributing article authors, planning the annual bridge photographic contest and writing feature articles for the magazine. The magazine (*Summer Edition*) enjoys a wide distribution between members of the Society and all attendees of the International Bridge Conference®.

The author is indebted to Mr. David Teorsky, General Manager of the *Engineers' Society of Western Pennsylvania*, for his and the *Society's* encouragement to publish and the Society's generous use of materials and images previously published in the *Pittsburgh Engineer*. The author also acknowledges the help of Mike Gaetano and Kristina Emmerson of the *Engineers' Society of Western Pennsylvania*. The author is indebted to Carrie Fox, Tarentum Borough Council and for their generous use of materials and images recently published in the *Tarentum Borough Magazine - Crossroads of the Allegheny Valley*.

The author extends special thanks to Elan Mizrahi for the splendid cover photography. And finally, the author is indebted to the Staff of Word Association Publishers, who without their help, this book could not have been published. This acknowledgement includes Tom Costello, Francine Costello, Jason Price and with special thanks to graphic artist, April Nelson whose book layout is most sincerely appreciated.

*Thomas Leech*

# TABLE OF CONTENTS

# INTRODUCTION

For every bridge there is a story.

For some it is their creator.

For some it is the unexpected.

For some it is a new understanding.

For some it is wind and rain.

For some it is the pounding of a train.

For others their story is a poem.

For some, there is tragedy, and others there is joy.

For some there is a sad ending, and for others a new beginning.

These are some of their stories.

# TO BUILD A BRIDGE

*bridge* - a structure carrying a road, path, railroad, or canal across a river, ravine, road, railroad, or other obstacle

*"The [builder] should be equipped with knowledge of many branches of study and varied kinds of learning, for it is by his judgement that all work done, by the other arts, is put to test. This knowledge is the child of practice and theory."*

**Vitruvius, De architectura (now known as The Ten Books of Architecture), Book 1, Chapter 1, c. 30 BCE**

... TO BUILD A BRIDGE ...

*Panther Hollow Bridge, Schenley Park, Pittsburgh, Pennsylvania
(Elan Mizrahi Photography)*

# How Far Would You Go To Build a Bridge?

*"In the rich quality of its simple, fine-textured masonry elements, in the lightness and purity of the arch, and in the sweeping curve of the parabola, ... the Panther Hollow Bridge ... represents the culmination of thirty years of progressive development in the arch, and there are few structures of its kind that can match it ..." Carl W. Condit American Building Art: The Nineteenth Century, 1960.*

In 1889, the City of Pittsburgh's first Public Works director, Edward Bigelow, had a grand vision for the city. In an era of dramatic change, industrial growth and seemingly unlimited potential on the horizon, Bigelow envisioned grand boulevards connecting the downtown business district with a large and connected park system. In 1889 there were no parks, there were no automobiles and street cars were not yet even a reality. But Bigelow's vision persisted and his first target for park development were farmlands immediately east of the growing urban sprawl, approximately 6 miles from downtown Pittsburgh. The farmlands, situated around a large ravine, noted for its lairs of wild panthers, were the land holdings of Mary (Elizabeth Croghan) Schenley, heiress to a large real estate fortune in Pittsburgh, Pennsylvania, and recently a widower who chose to live the remainder of her life in London, England, her adopted country.

The urban parks movement was underway in other major US cities in the mid-19th century. In this spirit, two decades earlier, Mary Schenley had offered the farmland tract for sale to the city; but this offer was withdrawn over a controversy whether the city should fund the purchase of park land. Aspirations for public parks in the City of Pittsburgh lay dormant for many years. Things changed rapidly in 1889.

In literally a race across the Atlantic, Edward Bigelow and Mary Schenley lawyer, Robert Carnahan, travelled from Pittsburgh to London, a distance of 4,000 miles, two days ahead of a businessman, who himself envisioned purchase of the large Schenley tract as opportunity for continued urban development. Winning the trans-Atlantic race by two days, Bigelow persuaded Mary Schenley to donate 300 acres of farmland to the City of Pittsburgh, for the development of its first and largest public park, a park named in her honor: Schenley Park.

*Newly Opened Panther Hallow Bridge, c. 1900, Photograph Courtesy of the Library of Congress*

*"The work of transforming what were for the most part stretches of vacant ground, broken here and there, with old buildings, into slightly pleasure grounds, traversed by shady drives and walks, connected by convenient bridges, has now advanced so toward completion that nature works visibly hand in hand with us in aiding to their beauty from year to year..." the words of Edward Bigelow, recorded in Pittsburgh Annual Report ... 1895.*

In September of the same year, construction began on the stone approach arches of the Panther Hollow Bridge. On August 1, 1896, the Panther Hollow Bridge, with its main steel truss-arched span of 360 feet spanning the deep ravine, was dedicated with limited fanfare, marking the completion of the first major bridge built in any Pittsburgh city park. The elegance of the steel arches, leaping out from the base of the stone approaches, represent a perfect harmony between structure and environment. In that same year, noted Scotsman, William Falconer was hired to transform the park and, especially the area in the immediate vicinity of the Panther Hollow Bridge, from a barren landscape to a horticultural gem by employing the most advanced standards of botany, horticulture and landscape architecture. Within the next 10 years, major park amenities, including the Phipps (horticultural) Conservancy, Nature Center, and electric fountain to the north of the bridge; band shell, oval and racetrack to the south of the bridge; bridle trails with modest but visually interesting tufa stone arches beneath the bridge; a lake to the east of the bridge; and acres of meticulously planned monocultures of trees and other plantings throughout the ravine, were finalized. In 1897, the first bronze sculpted panthers, the creation of Giuseppe Moretti, a locally prominent artist, were erected at the approaches to the bridges. The four, 1200-pound panther statues, guarding each corner of the bridge have become as symbolic of the bridge as is the main arch span.

*Panther Statue - one of the four Moretti panter statues guarding the Panther Hollow Bridge Photograph Courtesy of the Author*

"*The Panther Hollow Bridge's parabolic curves blended with the steep hillsides crossed by the structure, exemplifying the aesthetic concerns intrinsic to the parks movement. As a material, steel combined strength with flexibility, presenting a potent symbol of the new Pittsburgh elite whose growing fortunes derived from steel's versatility as a structural material … civic leaders such as …[Edward] Bigelow constructed physical bridges to turn their own vision of the [19th century] City Beautiful [Movement] into fact …*" HAER (Historical American Record) PA-489

Not only is the bridge, an architectural gem, but the ink drawings which created the bridge, represent a marriage of engineering and architecture with artistic training. The bridge elevation drawing includes a figure of a man with hat and walking stick appearing beneath the bridge, drawn in proportion with respect to scale. The illustration offers a subtle philosophical statement – as seen through the eyes of the 19th century – of the relationship of man, technology and nature, or in other words, the faith in human ability to improve upon nature. [From a twenty-first century perspective, this could be considered folly.]

The drawings also uniquely present the structural analysis of the three-hinged steel, deck arch in a completely graphical format, with "strains" [which we now call stresses] drawn to scale – a practice no longer of value with the high-speed computer. And the drawings include erection sketches of a massive falsework system, which filled the steep ravine with wooden trusses to support the four steel arches up to the point of erection closure.

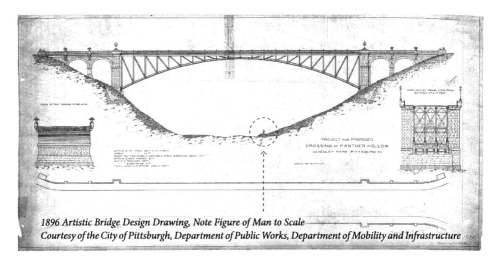

*1896 Artistic Bridge Design Drawing, Note Figure of Man to Scale*
*Courtesy of the City of Pittsburgh, Department of Public Works, Department of Mobility and Infrastructure*

*"In the end, our society will be defined not only what we create, but what we refuse to destroy." John Crittenden Sawhill, president and CEO of The Nature Conservancy and the 12th President of New York University*

One hundred years after its birth, the Panther Hollow Bridge faced deterioration with age and need for a well-conceived preservation. A bridge, which was designed for likely the largest expected loading of a paving machine, had seen the birth of the twentieth century and had experienced the loading of the automobile, the cement truck and the school bus. With concern for exhaustion of useful fatigue life and in places, corrosive deterioration, the bridge underwent a major rehabilitation and by 1998, the bridge was sensitively restored, consistent with its original historical context, and ready for the next 100 years.

Bridge as seen from Panther Hollow Lake (1927 photo) Courtesy of the City of Pittsburgh, Department of Public Works, Department of Mobility and Infrastructure

A footnote:

> "…. beauty, simplicity, rigidity, stable, practical, aesthetic … a beautiful bridge, larger than expected … it appears quite modern even though it was built in 1896 … I can visualize the member forces as traffic crosses the bridge! … a serene setting … It felt very secure …this assignment made me look at bridges differently "… Carnegie Mellon University Engineering Students, Department of Civil and Environmental Engineering

The above are the reactions of [the author's] engineering students who are assigned the task of analyzing the 1896 steel arch and expressing their impression of the structure as part of the Engineering Mechanics coursework curriculum. "Hands on" experience in a "real world" application of engineering principles prepares the next generation of engineers, who can quickly appreciate the work of our engineering forefathers, from many years ago.

Panther Hollow Bridge & Schenley Park (2020) Once (in 1896) a scene devoid of trees
Courtesy of the Author

# Bridges in the Wilderness – the Bridges of the National Road

*A leisurely day trip along U.S. 40 through the mountains of Western Maryland, the ridges and river valleys of Pennsylvania and West Virginia, or the farmlands of Ohio, will bring the twenty-first century traveler in close contact with the last visible vestiges of our nation's first national highway. These vestiges – the mile marker monuments, the bridges, the inns and tollhouses – are a reminder of the spirit of travel of our forefathers and remain an archeological record of the technologies of the day.*

## How it all began …

In 1818, the National Road, then known as the Cumberland Road, was opened to foot and stagecoach traffic. This was the first important road built in the country using federal funds. Its location, originally winding through the Allegheny Mountain wilderness, from the Chesapeake River in Cumberland, Maryland to the Ohio River at Wheeling, (then) Virginia, was selected by a group of Commissioners under the direction of Thomas Jefferson. A significant portion of the road's location was carefully selected utilizing natural topography to best form a route though the arduous mountain terrain. A significant portion of the road's alignment followed Native American trails such as the Mingo Trail and the old Braddock Trail. The latter was used by General Braddock and his young assistant, George Washington, during the pursuit of the French at Fort Duquesne (present day Pittsburgh), during the French and Indian Wars of the 1760's. In the 1820s, the road was extended to Illinois. The federal government turned the road over to the individual states in the 1830s due to costly maintenance. The states decided to collect fees, or tolls, from travelers to defray the cost, hence America's first toll road was born.

Present day Route 40 follows, and in many locations, lies in the same alignment as the original National Road. Remarkably, many of the bridges, inns and toll houses, built in the 1818-1840 era still remain – several in very close proximity to present day Route 40. Tollhouses, some of the grand inns and mileage markers have been restored along the corridor. As we consider the present-day complexities of commerce and utilization of our modern toll roads, it is interesting to reflect back on the technology of 200 years ago, at our nation's infancy, and consider the challenges facing the design and construction of bridges along this original National Road.

Our journey follows the original course of the National Road from the terminus of the C&O Canal in Cumberland and winds westward through the mountains and hill country of western Maryland, southwestern Pennsylvania, the panhandle of West Virginia and into the farmlands of Ohio. Along the way we will visit many unique and individual structures.

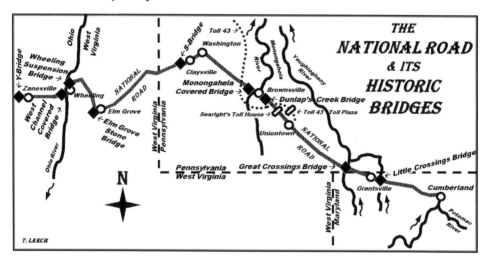

*The Early Bridges of the National Road*

## Little Crossings (of the Youghiogheny) – Casselman River Bridge

The National Road quickly rose from the lowlands of Cumberland, Maryland and ascended Big Savage Mountain, crossed the Eastern Continental Divide and faced its first formidable river crossing, then known as the "Little Crossings". The resulting 80-foot stone arch bridge, erected in 1813, was the largest stone arch in America at the time of construction and was continuously used from

1813 to 1933. The large span and high profile of the arch anticipated the C&O Canal coming through the mountains, passing alongside the river and gently moving canal boats under the bridge. This beautiful elliptical arch, now located in Casselman State Park, is a Registered National Historic Landmark.

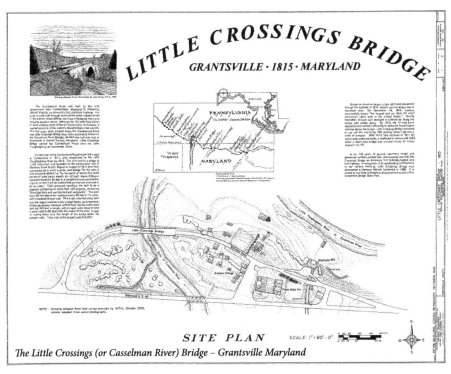

*The Little Crossings (or Casselman River) Bridge – Grantsville Maryland*

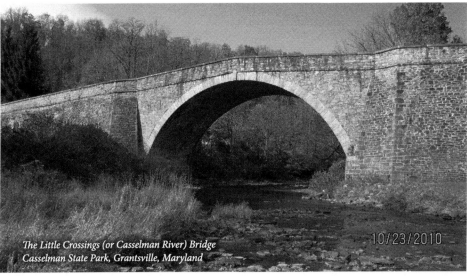

*The Little Crossings (or Casselman River) Bridge*
*Casselman State Park, Grantsville, Maryland*

# Somerfield (or "Great Crossings") Bridge

One large river valley penetrates the heart of the Allegheny Mountain range in southwestern Pennsylvania. Braddock's Trail forded this river at its shallowest point and the National Road constructed a handsome 40-foot high, 375-foot long three-span stone arch at this "Great Crossings" of the Youghiogheny River. In 1940, the river valley was submerged for flood control and recreational purposes and remnants of this once marvelous stone bridge and the ruins of the village of Somerfield are visible in November when the lake has been drained to its lowest point. In years of severe drought, one can see, on the eastern end of the bridge, the inscription: "Kinkead, Beck & Evans, builders, July 4th, 1818".

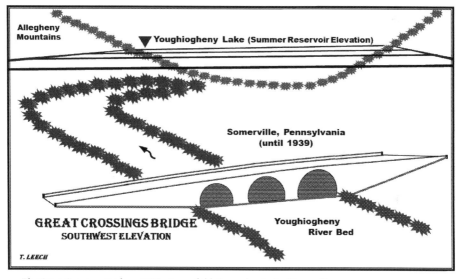

*The Great Crossings Bridge – 1939 - Somerfield, Pennsylvania (looking east)*
*Image based on early 20th century post card: The Bend in the Youghiogheny*

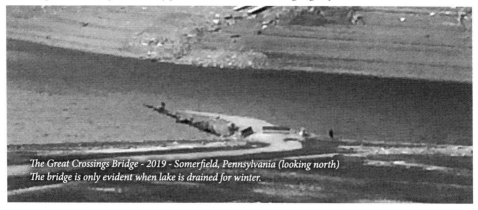

*The Great Crossings Bridge - 2019 - Somerfield, Pennsylvania (looking north)*
*The bridge is only evident when lake is drained for winter.*

## *Dunlap's Creek Bridge*

After penetrating the mountain barrier, the National Road made a beeline for the Monongahela River community of Brownsville, at that time largest city of western Pennsylvania. The Dunlap's Creek Bridge within the city of Brownsville, was as a scene of particularly unfortunate bridge accidents up through the year 1839, as several bridges crossed this small 80-foot gorge. The bridges included wooden bridges which burned and a chain suspension bridge, which collapsed under the weight of snow. In 1839, the use of an arched iron bridge was conceived by its designer, Army Corps of Engineers Capt. Richard Delafield, given its close proximities of the Brownsville Iron Foundries (which rivaled Pittsburgh's iron works at that time). The "Neck" (the nickname of downtown Brownsville) was crossed with America's first cast-iron bridge, which remains in vehicular traffic use to this day and is designated as a National Historic Civil Engineering Landmark.

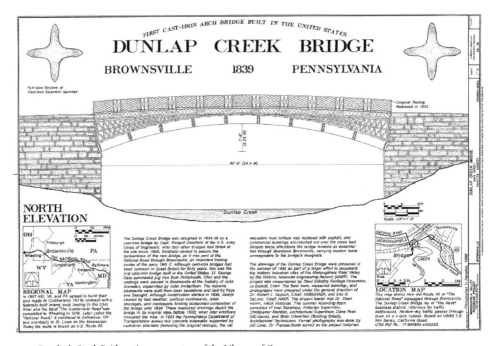

*Dunlap's Creek Bridge – image courtesy of the Library of Congress*

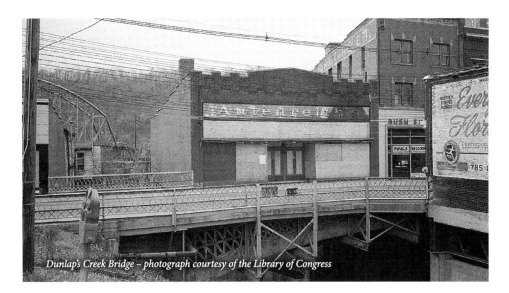

*Dunlap's Creek Bridge – photograph courtesy of the Library of Congress*

# Monongahela River Crossing

The Monongahela River was a laborious river crossing in the early days of the National Road; by 1830, the ferry was replaced with a three-span wooden covered bridge. This remarkable structure, with approximately 200-foot wooden arch spans, was the first bridge across a major river west of the Appalachian Mountains. In 1910, the bridge was declared an obstruction to river traffic and was pulled down by a cable wrapped around its timbers connected to a moving steamboat. The sound of cracking wood was heard for miles and spectators along the bank were soaked by the mighty splash!

*Monongahela Covered Bridge at Brownsville – photograph courtesy of the Library of Congress*

## "S" Bridge

As the toll road followed the winding ridges and valleys to the Ohio River, many small tributaries were crossed. As typical of the era, the streams were crossed in their shortest direction, regardless of the general path or direction of the roadway. An entire series of stone "S-bridges" were built along small tributaries, such as the "S-bridge" located 5 miles west of Washington, Pennsylvania over Buffalo Creek. For this two-span arch bridge, the main span was aligned at right angles to the stream; the minor span and approaches were aligned in an east to west direction of the roadway, confronting the likely weary traveler with a contorted "S" pathway.

S-Bridge, Claysville, Pennsylvania (looking west) - photograph courtesy of the Library of Congress

## Elm Grove Stone Bridge

As the National Road entered present-day West Virginia, it followed the tributary system of Wheeling Creek and crossed this branch of the Ohio River with a series of stone elliptical arches, unusual for their time of construction. Built in 1817, the elegant three-span Elm Grove Stone Bridge was then known as the Monument Place Bridge, due to bridge architect Moses Shepherd's nearby memorial to (U.S. Secretary of State) Henry Clay, for his support of the National Road. The bridge, spanning Little Wheeling Creek, is the oldest extant bridge in West Virginia and remains intact and viable to this day.

*Elm Grove Stone Bridge, c. — photograph courtesy of the Ohio County Public Library Archives, Wheeling, WV*

# Wheeling Suspension Bridge

Originally the National Road ended near the mouth of Wheeling Creek along the Ohio River, the destination for travelers continuing by water to the interior of the country. The City of Wheeling was quickly extended across the east (and main) channel of the Ohio River to Zane's Island (now known as Wheeling Island) by a 1,010-foot long suspension bridge; but is was not an easy task. The Commonwealth of Pennsylvania, led by Edwin M. Stanton (later to become Abraham Lincoln's Secretary of War), filed a suit in the U.S. Supreme Court to prevent construction because the bridge would obstruct river traffic. The designer, Charles Ellet, Jr., the father of suspension bridges (in the U.S.), pressed forward with the design and construction of this wrought iron structure and managed to complete and open the bridge in 1850. Stanton, upset about the bridge, drove the steamer "Hibernia No. Two" into the bridge to prove that the bridge was a hindrance. The court ordered Ellet to substantially raise his bridge, but he succeeded to have the bridge declared a post road, which had seniority over all transportation arteries. Tragically, after this fight, the suspension bridge collapsed when a severe gale induced undulatory motion in the superstructure on May 17, 1854. This increasing twisting motion caused by aeroelastic instability, directly led to collapse of the superstructure in a violent and sudden state. The superstructure was temporarily restored in forty days, entirely reconstructed in 1860, and in 1872, furthered strengthened with stay cables by John A. Roebling and Sons. The structure remains in service to this day.

*Wheeling Suspension Bridge, c. 1850's – before the storm - photograph courtesy of the Ohio County Public Library Archives, Wheeling, WV*

*Wheeling Suspension Bridge, c. 1886 – photograph courtesy of the Ohio County Public Library Archives, Wheeling, WV*

*Wheeling Suspension Bridge - present day with stay cables from 1872 rehabilitation – photograph courtesy of the Library of Congress*

# West Channel Covered Bridge (Zane's Crossing)

Zane's Island (presently Wheeling Island) was a strategic location for crossing the Ohio River. This large island made a natural crossing point for early settlers seeking a path to the west. From 1830, the Zane family maintained a ferry service across the east channel (which ended when the Wheeling Suspension Bridge was completed). Across the west channel of the Ohio River at Zane's Island, the Zane family constructed a wooden, covered toll bridge in 1836. The toll keeper lived on the bridge at the Ohio (western) side of the west channel of the river.

*West Channel Covered Bridge (Zane's Crossing) over the Ohio River – photograph courtesy of the Ohio County Public Library Archives, Wheeling, WV*

# Ohio and Beyond

As the National Road extended from the hilly provinces of western Ohio to the gently sloping farm country of eastern Ohio, Indian and Illinois, many bridge vestiges of the National Road era remain intact. These bridges included the Y-Bridge, spanning the confluence of Muskingham & Licking River in Zanesville, Ohio, the three-span stone arch in Blaine, Ohio and the "S"-bridges in Cambridge and New Concord, Ohio.

*Y-Bridge, Zanesville, Ohio – bridge splits in half in the middle of the river, hence the name "Y" Bridge – photograph courtesy of the Library of Congress*

## *Two Toll Roads Separated in Time*

The year was 1835. In that year the National Road was a disintegrating wooden plank roadway undulating to the natural contours of the region. As the roadway lay in disrepair, Maryland, Pennsylvania, (West) Virginia and Ohio, agreed to own, repair and toll the roadway in their respective states and the National Road was revitalized. The National Road brought commerce through the Alleghenies to the Ohio Valley and has been preserved as present-day US 40.

*The year - 1835:* The latitude is N39°-57'; the longitude is W79°-48'. The small octagonal red brick building lying at these coordinates is the Searight's Toll House, one of the many toll houses built at 15-mile intervals along the wooden plank roadway. The chain is down and lying above the roadway. The toll collector is staring at a seemingly endless line of patiently waiting wagoners, drovers with a variety of squeamish livestock, stage coaches with weary travelers and tired mail express riders. The wooden plank roadway is the National Road, open for business.

*Searight's Toll House, Fayette County, Pennsylvania*

*One hundred eighty years later:* The latitude is N39°-57', the longitude is W79°-48' – and at one mile to the east of this small octagonal building, now a National Historic Landmark, lies a state-of-the-art toll plaza, where EZ Pass truck and automobile drivers *slow down* to 55 mph to pass through the toll plaza. The road, Toll 43, follows the trace of the National Road for 17-miles of its northerly journey, from Uniontown, Pennsylvania, at the foot of the Allegheny Mountains, to Brownsville, Pennsylvania and the crossing of the Monongahela River.

*Toll 43 Toll Plaza, Fayette County, Pennsylvania – photograph courtesy of Gannett Fleming, Inc.*

Within those 17 miles of hilly, undulating terrain, the largest bridge of the 1835 National Road, intended for stage coaches, wagoners and drovers, was a single span, cast-iron arch bridge over Dunlap's Creek. And the formidable Monongahela River was traversed by ferry (and later a covered bridge). Today, in the same 17 miles, the expressway carefully follows the path of the National Road but the roadway soars over the myriad of stream dissected valleys, with 37 bridges, none of which are more impressive than the bridges over Dunlap's Creek and the Monongahela River.

*Viaduct (Toll 43) over Dunlap's Creek, Brownsville, Pennsylvania – photograph courtesy of Gannett Fleming, Inc.*

*Monongahela River Crossing (Toll 43), Brownsville, Pennsylvania – photo courtesy of Gannett Fleming, Inc.*

## Epilogue

Today, U.S. 40 extends from Atlantic City to San Francisco. In 2002, our first toll road earned the status of National Scenic All-American Byway, one of the highest honors bestowed on a traveled route. With its spectacular scenery, breathtaking bridges, and historic charm, the National Road possesses the unique ability to transport present-day society back into time. If by chance you travel on U.S. 40 in western Maryland, southwestern Pennsylvania, the West Virginia Panhandle or eastern Ohio, relive the birth of our transportation industry, and appreciate the milestones encountered along the way.

# *What Does It Take To Build A Bridge?*

" *[My soldiers] ... caused pairs of balks [i.e. wooden piles] a foot and half thick, sharpened a little way from the base and measured to suit the depth of the river ... These [were] lowered into the river by means of rafts and set fast and drove home by rammers; not ... straight up and down, but leaning forward at a uniform slope, so that they inclined in the direction of the stream. Opposite to these, again were planted two balks ... each pair, slanted against the force and onrush of the stream ... So, as they were ... clamped together, the stability of the structure was so great and its character such that, the greater the force and thrust of the water, the tighter were the balks held in lock ... so that if trunks of trees, or vessels, were launched by the natives to break down the structure, these fenders might lessen the force of such shocks, and prevent them from damaging the bridge ..."  from **Commentāriī dē Bellō Gallicō** (known in English as **the Gallic Wars**) by Julius Caesar, c. 50 BCE, commemorating the 10-day construction of a bridge across the Rhein River near present day Koblenz, Germany.*

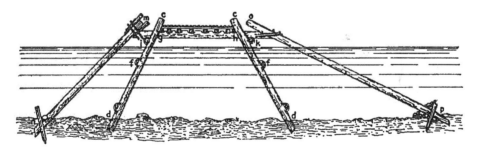

*Caesar's Bridge – c. 50 BCE – from the Ancient Engineers, DeCamp, 1966*

The first recorded engineering "journal article" describing bridge construction was not penned by an engineer or architect, but by a military commander. Written in a third person narrative, Julius Ceasar described battles, intrigues ... and bridge construction ... that took place in the nine years he spent fighting the Germanic and Celtic peoples in Gaul (modern day France, Belgium, Germany and Switzerland). This narrative, in vivid, yet simple and understandable language marks the beginning of recorded discourses documenting the skills of workers who build bridges.

# *The Power of the Triangle*

*The Tarentum Bridge*

**Triangle after triangle after triangle** – the dominating feature of the metal elements of the Tarentum Bridge, in Western Pennsylvania. Where did this notion of triangle, strength and long span bridge come from? The year is 1570; and at the height of the Renaissance, Italian architect, Andrea Palladio, wrote a small architectural composition, *"I quattro libri dell' Architecturea"* – translated: *The Four Books of Architecture*. In this writing, Palladio presented text, sketches and personnel interpretations of his *"inventioni"* - "inventions" - of wooden bridges he proposed to be built over small Italian streams. While it is not certain which, if any of these bridges, were actually built, these wooden bridge "inventions" were unique. Each bridge, though appearing quite differently, one from another, was formed by a series of wooden triangles, with rhythmic triangular patterns, repeating over and over again. Although more interested in form than strength, Palladio uncovered an important engineering principle: the triangle is a powerful engineering form. Palladio did not give a name to his "invention" and his idea of repeated triangles, uncovered by contemporaries, became slowly put into use in the roofs of cathedrals, but forgotten as a use in bridges until the 19th century. With modest success in wooden and iron bridges in the 19th century, the truss – by modern definition: a rigid framework of individual members connected to form a series of triangles - became the workhorse of long span bridge types in the 20th century. None is better exemplified than the 1952 Tarentum Bridge, spanning the Allegheny River, 22 river miles upstream from Pittsburgh at the Point. The bridge, with its beautifully curved steel profile, graces the Allegheny River and carries on the tradition of the "*inventioni*" of Palladio.

*Angelo Frederick became the first driver to cross the newly-minted Tarentum Bridge on Feb. 18, 1952*

*Concrete pouring on the approach from West Tarentum, June 11, 1951*

# CHAPTER 2

# ART & ARCHITECTURE

*art* - the expression or application of human creative skill and imagination, typically in a visual form

*architecture* - the style in which a structure is designed and constructed, especially with regard to a specific period, place or culture

*"Art is never finished, only abandoned." - Leonardo da Vinci*

# Art & Architecture

Salginatobelbrücke

The Salgina (Creek) Canyon Bridge
Schiers, Switzerland

Robert Mallard
Constructed 1930

Photos courtesy of the author.

The Salginatobel Bridge is considered a highlight of 20th Century bridge architecture. As an outstanding engineering feat and modern work of art, it has an almost magical attraction to experts and artists alike since its completion in 1930.

In 1991, The American Society of Civil Engineers declared this exceptional bridge a WORLD MONUMENT, one of thirty such structures, such as the Eiffel Tower and Statue of Liberty, with the same designation.

# The Poem And The Bridge

*Longfellow Bridge looking northwest, courtesy of Library of Congress*

*As the clocks were striking the hour,*

*And the moon rose o'er the city,*

*Behind the dark church-tower.*

And so begins the words of the Poem entitled *The Bridge* by Henry Wadsworth Longfellow (from the book of poetry: *The Belfry of Bruges and Other Poems* ). In the late evening in 1845, a thirty-eight year old Longfellow left his Cambridge Massachusetts residence, walked along Main Street, and heading eastward, ascended the bridge over the Charles River. From the deck of the wooden trestle Wadsworth, in a moment of solemn reflection, contemplated these words.

*I saw her bright reflection*

*In the waters under me,*

*Like a golden goblet falling*

*And sinking into the sea.*

**37**

*And far in the hazy distance*

*Of that lovely night in June,*

*The blaze of the flaming furnace*

*Gleamed redder than the moon.*

The city of Boston that he looked upon to the east was quite different than the Boston of today. To the east, with moon rising, he could make the outline of North Boston and perhaps the steeple of the Old North Church. To the southeast he would look up Beacon Hill ascending from the Commons and see the Massachusetts State House, declared several years later by Oliver Wendell Holmes, a noted American physician and author, to be the "hub of the universe." Longfellow would not have viewed the State House adorned with its characteristic gilded golden copper dome forged by Paul Revere, but instead a dome simply painted a dull stone gray. To the south there would be no thriving Back Bay community, just a wide expanse of tidal marshlands. Perhaps he could make out the silhouette of the recently built milldam, a toll road, the future extension of Beacon Street and at that time a narrow embankment built in these tidal marsh lands in an effort to capture and release tidal waters for hydroelectric power. The filling of the estuary behind the milldam would not begin for more than 10 years in the future and would take over 35 years to complete. Under his feet he could watch the ebb and flow of the tide. The tide would rise and fall in these waters for another 65 years, before the Charles River Dam was constructed, converting this tidal estuary into a fresh water basin.

*Among the long, black rafters*

*The wavering shadows lay,*

*And the current that came from the ocean*

*Seemed to lift and bear them away;*

*As sweeping and eddying through them,*

*Rose the belated tide,*

*And, streaming into the moonlight,*

*The seaweed floated wide.*

Although Cambridge lay distance wise only one mile away from Boston, travel by land was lengthy requiring a circuit run around the Charles River estuary and entering Boston by the "neck", a narrow 120 foot wide strip of land well to the southwest of the city. The first river crossing at the eastern end of Main Street site was a ferry with service first recorded in 1630, the year the city of Cambridge was founded. The bridge, upon which Longfellow was standing, was built in 1793 with pine piles hand driven into the mud flats to create a wooden trestle bridge. The bridge, originally called the West Boston Bridge, had oils lights, a draw span and some relentless pine worms who, unbeknownst to Longfellow, were eating the bridge away underneath his feet as he contemplated his poem.

> *And like those waters rushing*
> *Among the wooden piers,*
> *A flood of thoughts came o'er me*
> *That filled my eyes with tears.*
> *How often, oh, how often,*
> *In the days that had gone by,*
> *I had stood on that bridge at midnight*
> *And gazed on that wave and sky!*

What Longfellow could not see coming was a grand steel and stone structure, replacing his pine worn trestle, that would inexorably link the cities of Boston and Cambridge and for years to come would define the character of the Charles River. Longfellow's wooden trestle was rebuilt in 1858; however, this second wooden trestle structure was short lived. Although sited for horse drawn trolleys, the bridge was too narrow to permit both trolleys and horse draw carriages and ill-considered for the coming electrified "rapid" transit system that was making a nationwide debut in Boston in the 1890s.

> *How often, oh, how often,*
> *I had wished that the ebbing tide*
> *Would bear me away on its bosom*

*O'er the ocean wild and wide!*

*For my heart was hot and restless,*

*And my life was full of care,*

*And the burden laid upon me*

*Seemed greater than I could bear.*

The 1890s were an exciting time in the city of Boston. In response to the grid-lock, created by a pre-revolutionary war street pattern and a busting density of horse-drawn wagons, electric streetcars and pedestrians, the world's fifth and the country's first subway was constructed for a one and one-half mile distance under Tremont Street in 1895. (Tremont and Beacon Streets lie at the eastern and western borders of Boston Commons, respectively.) By 1898 the need to extend the underground subway from the city of Boston to the city of Cambridge became evident and was the catalyst for the construction of a new bridge across the Charles River. In June of 1898, bridge commissioners, comprising the mayors of the cities of Boston and Cambridge, appointed William Jackson, Chief Engineer and appointed Edmund M. Wheelwright as Consulting Architect. At that time all bridges in the region were pile bridges and were considered "unsightly" and generally not suitable for electrified trolleys. With a look to the future, both gentlemen were immediately dispatched to Europe to make a survey of notable bridges constructed in steel and stone which could serve as design models for a new bridge across the Charles River. One year later, legislation was enacted for the construction of a new bridge paid for by both cities and the newly formed Boston Elevated Railway Company.

*But now it has fallen from me,*

*It is buried in the sea;*

*And only the sorrow of others*

*Throws its shadow over me.*

*Yet whenever I cross the river*

*On its bridge with wooden piers,*

*Like the odor of brine from the ocean*

*Comes the thought of other years.*

The new bridge, to be called the Cambridge Bridge, was originally conceived as a series of arched steel approach spans and stone foundations, with flanking, back to back, dual mid-river draw-spans. This concept was the result of an exhaustive two year study considering various alternatives of masonry and steel structures based on the European studies. The War Department (predecessor to the Army Corps of Engineers) insisted on a draw span structure, not strictly for general navigational purposes but in consideration of the movement of the navy and the defense of the city. As this design progressed, a unified concept developed that included a single massive stone tower at mid-river adjacent to the two draw spans, one draw span for upstream and the second draw span for downstream river traffic. This massive stone tower was detailed to skillfully hide the rotating mechanisms of both draw spans.

> *And I think how many thousands*
> *Of care-encumbered men,*
> *Each bearing his burden of sorrow,*
> *Have crossed the bridge since then.*
> *I see the long procession*
> *Still passing to and fro,*
> *The young heart hot and restless,*
> *And the old subdued and slow!*

With one of the financiers of the project being the Boston Elevated Railway Company, a bridge solution with draw spans containing an overhead electrified catenary line became untenable. After much consternation between the city governments and the War Department, the United States Congress enacted special legislation to build a "draw-less" bridge. The legislation was signed by President McKinley in March 1900, only 18 months before his untimely death. Quickly a new design concept was borne that included two signature architectural elements. Firstly, a long vertical crest profile was defined to optimize clearance of the main span over the tidal waters of the Charles River. And secondly and more important architecturally, the previously envisioned single stone tower of the central span (initially conceived as an adroit means of hiding the lifting machinery) was modified to become two distinctive stone towers symmetrically flanking the main river span. This duality has led to the popular nickname of the "salt and pepper shaker" bridge due to the distinctive shape of the towers. Additionally, the towers were fitted with sculptured motifs of Viking ships, alluding to a supposed Viking navigator entering the Charles River in discovery of America.

*And forever and forever,*

*As long as the river flows,*

*As long as the heart has passions,*

*As long as life has woes;*

*The moon and its broken reflection*

*And its shadows shall appear,*

*As the symbol of love in heaven,*

*And its wavering image here.*

*Looking East*

In 1906 the Cambridge Bridge was opened to both electrified railway, carriage and foot traffic. In 1927, the Cambridge Bridge was renamed as the Longfellow Bridge by the Massachusetts General Court in honor of Henry Wadsworth Longfellow, who contemplated the poem, *The Bridge,* while standing on the old West Boston Bridge. And after more than one hundred years since its conception, the bridge remains an architectural heritage and an icon of the Charles River.

# A Footnote

For a detailed history of the construction of the present Longfellow Bridge, with the most interesting construction drawings and photos, see the Cambridge Bridge Commission Report – Construction of the Cambridge Bridge, 1909. The 363 page report can be viewed on-line (and downloaded in pdf).

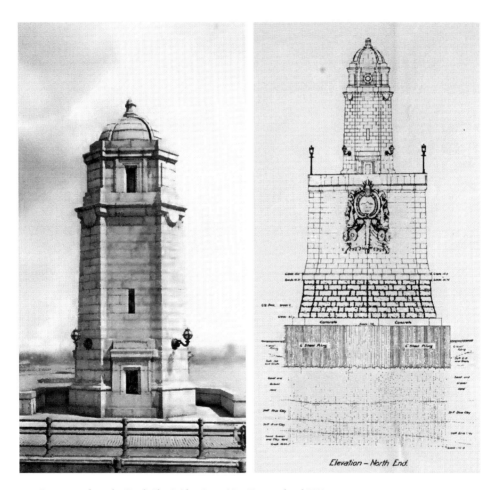

*Images are from the Cambridge Bridge Commision Report, dated 1909*

# A Leisurely Walk Along the Seine River

**Fifteen Beautiful Bridges of Paris . . .**
**Engineering, Architecture & Arts**

*Take one sunny day, put on a pair of comfortable sneakers, prepare to walk five miles and see some of the most beautiful bridges in the world. Exit Paris's Metro line 6 near the eastern boundary of the city, amble downstream along the river bank and reenter Metro line 6 near the western boundary of the city. Along the way, enjoy fifteen of the most unique expressions of engineering, architecture and arts reflected in Parisian bridges.*

The Seine River, with its headwaters at in the Langres plateau in eastern France, 50 miles from the Atlantic, meanders through the bowl shaped Paris Basin on its way to the sea. The Paris Basin lies in a relatively quiet tectonic region, and for millennia the Paris Basin has experienced rising and falling oceans through periods of global warming and cooling. The climax of epochs of glacial cooling was punctuated by the flow of swift melt waters in the Seine, that reduced the landscape to level terrain interrupted by small resistant promontory ridges. On a large island in the middle of the river, a small fishing village was born, bridges were built and then a large city arose. Today, as the Seine enters Paris, it flows under the most architecturally interesting and, in some cases, most historically significant bridges in the world. Paris is called the City of Lights. It could equally be named the City of Beautiful Bridges.

On the Left Bank of the Seine (heading downstream) lays the seat of French education and arts. On the Right Bank lays the seat of French government. The bridges spanning the Seine literally and symbolically link arts, education and government. The bridges of the Seine are a fusion of engineering, architecture and arts combining well proportioned structural forms, grace and symbolism.

While geography has provided the location for the bridges of the Seine, history has provided rich context for an understanding of the fusion of form, art and symbolism of these bridges. It is believed that a settlement on the site of modern-day Paris was founded about 250 BCE by a Celtic tribe called the Parisii, who established a fishing village traditionally assumed be located on the Île de la Cité, the largest island on the Seine within the city. Since that time the city has developed and prospered. While images of the Bastille, the guillotine and the first revolution of 1789 color our imagination as an emerging French Republic, there are other equally important dated milestones in history which have had a direct effect on the design of many of the Seine River Bridges. These milestones include the formation of modern Pairs in 1853 where, under Napoleon (III)'s rule, Prefect Baron Haussmann modernized the City to a drastic extent, demolishing much of the old city and replacing it with a network of wide, straight boulevards and radiating circuses. This was followed by the Third Republic, formed after the Prussian war of 1870 where the Belle Époque ("Beautiful Era") period began. This period was characterized by new technological and medical discoveries and optimisms, art nouveau architecture and artistic movements like impressionism, all of which had a direct influence on the bridges of that era and beyond.

Paris has 37 bridges which cross the Seine, of which four are pedestrian only and two are rail bridges. Three link Ile Saint-Louis (the smaller island), eight link Ile de la Cite (the larger island) and one links the two islands to each other. Fifteen of the bridges represent the finest expression of Parisan bridge architecture. To capture the best light on each of the bridges, let us begin the five mile walking tour starting in the mid-morning on the eastern side of Paris and travel from east to west. One half mile east of Metro Line 6 Station (Quai de la Gare), our walking journey begins as we walk along the orderly and well developed waterfront. On this small journey we will stop at fifteen beautiful bridge sites along the way.

**Bridge No. 1 : Pont de Tolbiac** – a robust, classically styled series of uniform masonry elliptical arches: The bridge was completed in 1882, built in a wave of urbanization of eastern Paris. The five-arched masonry bridge was constructed by the engineers Bernard and Pérouse after a more ambitious design by Gustave

Eiffel was refused. It was hit by a downed British plane in 1943, but survives today unimpeded and ever beautiful.

**Bridge No. 2: Simone de Beauvoir footbridge** – a light and delicate steel, lenticular arch-stress ribbon, which in illusion, appears as if it is hanging without visible support: The lenticular structure with five separate walking levels was constructed by Eiffel Constructions Métalliques in the Alsace. The central span of the bridge (named the peltinée) was transported by canal, through the North Sea, through the English Channel, then along the French rivers to its destination, and was hoisted in place in two hours on January 29, 2006, around three o'clock in the morning. The pedestrian bridge is named after France's first influential feminist.

**Bridge No. 3: Pont de Bercy** – a series of elliptical masonry arches with a Roman styled concrete aqueduct cast upon the superstructure: The original ferry at the site was replaced by a suspension bridge in 1832, then reconstructed as a stone structure in 1864. The bridge was further enlarged in 1904 to support the metro with an aqueduct styled structure cast upon the superstructure. The bridge was subsequently symmetrically widened in 1992 by reinforced concrete and dressed in a stone façade to match the original (1864) structure.

**Bridge No. 4: Pont Charles de Gaulle** – a monolithic steel box girder with a "disappearing" design: In 1986, the Council of Paris conducted a European-wide competition to determine the best project design for the site of a new bridge. At the conclusion of the competition, the concept set forth was based on the rationale that the choice did not detract from the aesthetic exterior of the nearby downstream lenticular Viaduc d'Austerlitz and that it discretely preserves the existing view of the river. In fact from certain perspectives, the bridge literally "disappears" from view.

**Bridge No. 5: Viaduc d'Austerlitz** – a braided steel arch with a unique Belle Époque expression: In 1903 the Building Society (La Societé de Construction de Levallois-Perret) proposed a bridge with a span reaching 460 feet, which was a record for Parisian bridges at the time. The completed metro viaduct consists of an interwoven parabolic steel arch and separate steel arch defined by a cubic parabola joined together at three distinct locations - two at the intersection with the deck and one at the crown. The steel arches are fitted with marine-themed reliefs, including dolphins, seashells and seaweeds. Near the footings, the arches are etched with figures of the Parisian Coat of Arms, which symbolizes steadfastness. Playful zodiac symbols adorn the approach columns – a common theme throughout the city.

rance

**Bridge Nos. 6A & 6B: Pont de Sully** – a series delicate cast iron arches flanked by stout masonry arches: A pair of pedestrian suspension bridges originally connected the left bank of the Seine with the right bank across the eastern tip of the iÎle St. Louis (smaller island). After destruction of the left bank bridge during the revolution in 1848 and collapse of the right bank bridge due to cable corrosion in 1872, the current bridges were built in 1876 under Prefect Baron Haussmann's modernization of the city. One bridge, connecting the island with the right bank (the Passerelle Damiette), is comprised of contrasting cast iron and masonry arches. A separate bridge between the island and the left bank (the Passerelle de Constantine) is a series of cast iron arches.

**Bridge Nos. 7A & 7B: Pont Neu** – a series of continuous, short span stone arches: With the corner stone laid in 1578, and a long delay due to the Wars of Religion, the bridge was inaugurated in 1607. As the oldest standing bridge crossing the Seine, the bridge was styled a series of repeating, small span stone arches following Roman engineering precedent. Its name was given to distinguish it from older bridges that were lined on both sides of the river. At the time of construction it was the only Parisian bridge that did not have houses built upon it, presumably to retain an unobstructed view of the King's castle (presently the Louvre). Standing by the western tip of the Ile de la Cite, the island in the middle of the river that was the heart of medieval Paris, the bridge connects the Rive Gauche (left bank) and the Rive Droite (right bank). A major restoration of was begun in 1994 and was completed in 2007, the year of its 400th anniversary.

**Bridge No. 8: Passerelle des Arts** – an airy, light and delicate series of small span steel arches symbolically and physically connecting the Institut de France (left bank) and the central square of the palais du Louvre (right bank): The Passerelle des Arts (bridge of the arts) was originally built in 1804, initially constructed in cast iron and conceived to resemble a suspended garden, with trees, banks of flowers, and benches. Suffering damage due to aerial bombardments in WW I & WWII and subsequent ship collision, Paris's first iron bridge partially collapsed in 1977. The new pedestrian bridge was re-built in 1984 "identically" according to the early 19th century plans except that there are now seven steel arch spans instead of the original nine cast iron arch spans.

**Bridge No. 9: Pont Royal** – a majestic series of stone arches: A 15 span wooden arch bridge was the first bridge constructed at the site in 1632, replacing a ferry that offered the first crossing in 1550. After fires and two floods, the later destroying the bridge, the present masonry arches were built in 1689. The bridge, situated in close proximity to the Louvre Palace as well as financed by and subsequently named by the King Louis XIV, underwent a reconstruction in 1850 (after the 1848 revolution). In 1939, it was classified as an historical monument.

**Bridge No. 10: Passerelle de Solférino** – an unusual architectural expression that requires some study to properly identify the supporting steel arch: Originally constructed as a cast iron bridge in 1861, and later replaced by a steel pedestrian bridge in 1961 and subsequently demolished, the new Passerelle de Solférino, supported by a pair of variable width arches, was constructed in 1999, crossing the Seine with a single span. This steel bridge is architecturally unique and partially covered which gives it a light and warm appearance. In 2006, on the centenary of his birth , the bridge was renamed Passerelle Léopold Sédar Senghor in honor of the first president of Senegal, who as a Senglaise poet, was the first African to sit as a member of the French Academy ( Académie française).

**Bridge No. 11: Pont Alexandre III** – an ornate, flat steel arch, best illustrating the fusion of engineering, architecture and art in Parisian bridge design: Regarded as the most ornate and extravagant bridge in Paris, the bridge, with its exuberant Art Nouveau lamps, cherubs, nymphs and winged horses at either end, was built in 1900 and named after Tsar Alexander III. Its construction was considered a marvel of 19th century engineering. Four gilt-bronze statues of Fames watch over the bridge, supported on a massive 55-foot socles. At the centers of the arches are copper castings representing the Nymphs of the Seine with the arms of France, and the Nymphs of the Neva with the arms of Imperial Russia.

**Bridge No. 12: Pont de L'Alma** – two span, steel, asymmetric box girder: At the site, a symmetric bridge was initially constructed in 1856. The original structure, containing ornate statues at each of 4 river piers, was considered unsafe after 30 inches of settlement occurred. The bridge was reconstructed in 1974 and styled deliberately in an asymmetric span arrangement, the only such arrangement of a river crossing in Paris, where all other structures follow well ordered rules of symmetry. With the 1974 construction, the statue of Zouave was retained. The bridge takes its name from the battle of Alma, where the French defeated the Russian army. It was the first war in which the Zouaves (the Papal Army) took part; hence the statue of the Zouave at the bridge. The statue was used to measure the height of the water; in the 1910 record flood, it reached the Zouave's beard.

**Bridge No. 13: Passerelle Debilly** – a "temporary" steel arch: In order to accommodate visitor traffic to the 1900 World's Fair across the Seine, the General Commissioner of the Exposition approved the construction of a "provisional" footbridge, intended for removal at the close of the exhibition. Built on a metallic framework resting on two stone piers at the riverbanks, the structure was initially decorated with dark green ceramic tiles arranged in a fashion that suggests the impression of waves. In 1941, the footbridge was characterized by the president of the architectural society as a "forgotten accessory of a past event" and strongly considered for demolition; however, with the onset of WWII all demolition plans were abandoned. Its distinctive shape has historical and architectural merit and the bridge was eventually included in the supplementary registry of historical monuments in 1966.

**Bridge No. 14: Pont d'Iéna** – stone arch ordered to be built by degree of Napoléon: This bridge which leads to the Eiffel Tower (left bank) coming from the Trocadéro (the wide esplanade on the right bank), was built in 1814. It was named after the German city of Jena (Iéna in French) where Napoléon had defeated the Prussian army in 1806. The statues, which were added in 1853, include a Gallic warrior, a Celtic warrior, a Roman warrior and an Arab warrior. In anticipation of the 1937 World's Fair, the bridge was widened using cast in place concrete construction, the bridge was faced with stone and the statues were repositioned. The bridge has been part of the supplementary registry of historic monuments since 1975.

**Bridge No. 15: Pont de Bir-Hakeim** – a pair of three span steel trusses connecting the right bank, the island of swans (île des Cygnes ) and the left bank: Completed in 1905, replacing a bridge erected at the site in 1878, the truss's diagonals are hidden from view by placement of an ornamental fascia metal façade to give the appearance of a sleek arch structure. The metal facade of the bridge is decorated at the (false) arch spring lines with castings of allegorical figures and the tip of the island (at the bridge mid-point) has widened plaza which is adorned with a bronze ornamental statue "reaching out" to the Eiffel Tower. The bridge has two levels: one for motor vehicles and pedestrians, and the upper level, a metro viaduct supported by metal colonnades, except where it passes over the île des Cygnes, where it rests on a masonry arch. Originally named Viaduc de Passy, it was renamed in 1949 after the Battle of Bir-Hakeim where French troops resisted Italian and German forces in 1942.

From the Pont de Bir-Hakeim, it is but a short walk to the Metro Line 6 Station (Bir-Hakeim), and as our walking journey ends, we leave the waterfront and end our journey to the fifteen beautiful bridge sites, best representing the Parisian fusion of engineering, architecture and arts.

*Paris at Twilight*
*Photo Courtesy of Author*

# The Bridges of the Merritt Parkway

## A Blend of Rustic and Art Deco Expression

*Aerial View of the Merritt Parkway, looking west, Fairfield Rest Area, Connecticut*
*Photography courtesy of Library of Congress*

On June 29, 1938, the architectural vision of the forty-six year old George Dunkelberger was finally realized as the first section of the Merritt Parkway was opened from Greenwich to Norwalk Connecticut. The road, a limited access highway, conceived as a bypass for Route 1, was considered a model of its day, most notably due to the architectural qualities of its more than 60 bridges. Route 1, originally called the Post Road or Kings Highway, was considered the gateway from New York City to New England. The Merritt Parkway became a second gateway. The parkway's undulating profile follows the gentle contours of the Connecticut landscape and the tree-lined, wide right of way presents a continuous visual buffer from nearby population centers. By design, there were no at grade intersections, with interchanges and grade separations for all overpassing and underpassing roadways and passenger rail lines. Completed in six years by 1940, the Merritt Parkway stands as Connecticut's greatest Depression-era public works project, employing over 2,000 workers.

The Merritt Parkway is characterized by a conscious design effort to create an ever changing picturesque appearance through well conceived structural and landscaping design. And the more than 60 concrete and steel, rigid frame and arch bridges are the celebrated features of the parkway, each individually styled and purposefully developed. Each of the bridges crossing the parkway is individually unique in its architectural character. The styles, while rustic, incorporate the art deco motifs popular at the time of construction.

In 1931, the Connecticut Highway Department assembled a team of specialists who traveled throughout the northeast to systematically and comprehensively study all roads and parkways under construction in efforts to surpass the accomplishments of all others. The team included Leslie Sumner, chief structural engineer, A. Earl Wood, engineer of roadside development, W. Thayer Chase, landscape architect and most notably, architect George Dunkelberger, who designed the unique and individualized finishes for each of the bridges. George Dunkelberger would also serve as site coordinator for the parkway. Certainly imagination was in play with the various architectural designs of George Dunkelberger, with some designs evoking mid-evil sentiments while others evoking modern and futuristic (for the time) elements. When completed the Parkway would achieve its intended goal of scenic motoring (at a designed speed of 45 mph). The Merritt Parkway may be considered the apex of the era of scenic motorways with its bridges as its crowning achievement.

The structurally efficient rigid frame was the perfect structural form for low clearance modest span structures. While most of the structures are constructed from cast in place concrete, several of the overpasses are supported by a slender steel rigid frame skeleton covered in a veneer of unusual surface treatments. The Art Deco theme is interesting and variant throughout the parkway. Even the most modern of rehabilitations and reconstructions of the bridges have held strictly to the tradition and style of George Dunkelberger. Much of the architectural expression can be witnessed closely by driving over any of the bridges where you are greeted with unusual railing treatments and in some cases unusual ornamentation such as flower boxes. With careful observation the drivers and passengers of the parkway can view unusual motifs cast into the surface features of the wing walls and girder spans. As one travels the parkway, anticipation builds, from one bridge to the next, surmising what new architectural expression will be revealed in the next overpassing bridge.

So, drive the parkway eastbound as I did on one cold and clear January day. Enter the Parkway at the Connecticut state line in early afternoon, when the sun is at your back, and watch the light and shadow dance before your eyes as you pass under each bridge, quietly anticipating the next bridge to enjoy. And enjoy the postcards I found along the way.

# Harmony & Height – Some Beautiful Bridge Settings in Western Pennsylvania

" *... architecture is the masterly, correct and magnificent play of masses brought together in light ...*" Le Corbusier

In the 1920's, Swiss-French architect and prolific writer, Le Corbusier (his name a pseudonym), became an advocate of new concepts of architecture in a series of critical articles published in *L'Esprit Nouveau*. In 1923, Le Corbusier fused these articles into a book entitled *Vers Une Architecture (Towards a New Architecture),* where he laid out the principles of "modern" architectural expression. When applied to rational design, his vision integrated fields of architecture and engineering into a single objective. In this "modern" approach, *form follows function.* Western Pennsylvania affords an opportunity to illustrate these principles on a grand scale. The best illustration of theses principles is the uniting of architecture and nature, with cantilevered concrete slabs suspended over a waterfall in Frank Lloyd Wright's Fallingwater (1937). Following this lead, many bridges constructed in western Pennsylvania in the latter half of the 20th century and early 21st century live by these principles.

*Fallingwater, Mill Run, PA – photograph courtesy of the author*

## The Setting

Who does not like to sit upon a high hill at sunset and gaze off in a distance and view a pleasant and interesting setting? Le Corbusier's father frequently took him into the mountains around the town. He would later write, "… we were constantly on mountaintops; we grew accustomed to a vast horizon…"

Western Pennsylvania lies in a unique geographic and geological setting – with myriads of stream dissected valleys, running *hither and yon*, seemingly in haphazard directions. Hills and valleys are everywhere – north-south and east-west directions become confused. If we step back a moment, we are quick to realize that the tops of all hills lie, with small deviation, at the same elevation above sea level.  And we quickly realize that those, who reside there, live in a plateau, dominated by an intricate, branching pattern of stream valleys following a tortured path eventually leading to the Ohio River Valley and then on to the Gulf of Mexico. Geologists call Western Pennsylvania the Appalachian Plateau, a fitting description for there are no hills, only valleys. But what an interesting place to build bridges.

The span of the large valleys and steep sided river banks presents opportunities for tall bridges and an interesting integration of the principles of architecture and engineering that Le Corbusier laid out in the early 1900s. The result, aesthetic bridges – bridges with both harmony and height.

## Architecture and Engineering

Contemplating a structure which is both functional and in harmony with its surroundings can be both challenging and rewarding if three architectural principles are considered as the design process unfolds. For as in a beautiful tune of music, an interplay of three harmonies in a bridge's form can result in a tuneful melody of proportion, perspective and light.

## Consideration of Proportion

*"A regulating line is a means to an end ... Its choice and the modalities of expression given to it are an integral part of the architectural creation ..."* Le Corbusier

With careful attention paid to the proportions of rise and span, tall slender viaducts, with careful repetition of form, highlight an uncluttered an orderly landscape and provide an open valley that allows light to pass through. With proper attention to ratio, the curved geometries of arches or rigid frame structures provide pleasing open spaces beneath the bridge, with the sense that the bridge is organically growing out of the surrounding hills – and is in essence a part of the terrain. Hence, a visual cohesion between bridge and valley surroundings results.

## Consideration of Perspective

*" ... Working by calculation, engineers employ geometric forms, satisfying our eyes by their geometry and our understanding by their mathematics ... their work is the direct line good art ..."* Le Corbusier

No structure is ever perceived as a two-dimensional object. We make drawings in two dimensions, but we live and sense in a three-dimensional world. In the three-dimensional world, straight lines remain straight lines, oblique perhaps, but still straight lines when viewed in perspective. Curved lines, for instance simple curves or parabolas, taken on mathematically complex, indefinable, and visually appealing shapes as they diverge to a common vanishing point. And as one's perspective changes relative to a structure, the bridge attains a sense of dynamic freedom. And as one winds down a steep valley, an opportunity develops to view each element of the structure from numerous, diverse and panoramic perspectives – and elements with proper consideration of perspective take on new and interesting forms.

## Consideration of Light

*" ... Our eyes are constructed to enable us to see forms in light: light and shade reveal these forms ... Primary forms are beautiful forms they can be clearly appreciated ..."*
*Le Corbusier*

Bridge elements with linear and congruent forms, such as tall pier shafts, are enhanced by ambient light in a number of ways. The flat surfaces are highly reflective and provide a canvas for the display of sunlight and shadows. Crisp edges and accent indentions distinctively divide the surfaces, separating the light from the dark, and give the viewer a clear sense of depth. Toward nightfall, when the suns rays hit a structure at a lower angle, the flat surfaces are illuminated like no other time of the day. The late shadows of the hills provide contrast that accents the flat surfaces, revealing their form. These optical effects heighten the sensitivity of the viewer to the object, enhancing one's appreciation of the overall design of the structure.

## Illustrations

Valley settings present unique opportunities for the development of bridge designs which can, by efficient structural forms, produce extremely graceful structures. The efficient structural forms include slender, long span, girder viaducts, slender arch forms and rigid (K) frame constructions. Creating structures that are both functional and in harmony to their surroundings can be both challenging and rewarding.

*Bloomfield Bridge, City of Pittsburgh, PA*

Joe Montana Bridges (Toll 43), Washington County, PA

Oakland Avenue Rigid Frame, Sharon, PA

Clarion River Bridge (US322), Clarion, PA

Evergreen Rigid Frame Overpass, Pittsburgh, PA

Hulton Bridge, Oakmont, PA

# CHAPTER 3

# THE CABLE

*cable* - a wire rope of great tensile strength

*"But even if a person were ignorant of such things, the sight of a moving train held aloft above the great gorge at Niagara by so delicate a contrivance was, in the 1860's, nothing short of miraculous. The bridge seemed to defy the most fundamental laws of nature. Something so slight just naturally ought to give way beneath anything so heavy. That it did not seemed pure magic."*

*David McCullough, from The Great Bridge: The Epic Story of the Building of the Brooklyn Bridge, describing an impression of the Niagara Falls Suspension Bridge which stood from 1855 to 1897 as it crossed the Niagara River. The bridge described, designed by John Augustus Roebling, was the world's first working railway suspension bridge.*

# The Cable

*Millau Viaduct*
*Tarn River Valley*
*near Millau, France*
*Constructed 2004*

*This Cable-Stayed Bridge, with the tallest tower reaching 1,104 feet above the valley floor, was the tallest bridge in the world at the time of construction.*

# Harmonious Rhythm – Bridges with Cables

*"Eurythmy [or harmonious rhythm] is beauty and fitness in the adjustments of the members. This is found when the members of a work are of a height suited to their breadth, of a breadth suited to their length, and, in a word, when they all correspond symmetrically." (Marcus) Vitruvius (Pollio) – Book 1, Chapter 2, THE FUNDAMENTAL PRINCIPLES OF ARCHITECTURE (Vitruvius was a noted 1ˢᵗ Century BCE author, architect, civil and military engineer whose works were rediscovered in the Renaissance and influenced the works of da Vinci and Michelangelo.)*

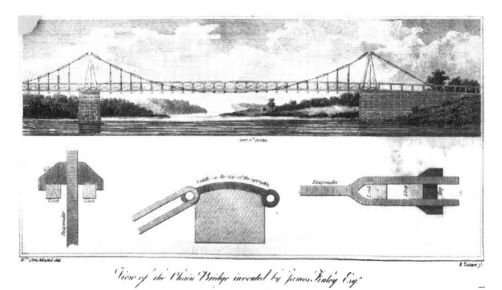

*View of the Chain Bridge Invented by James Finley Esq. aka "The Chain Bridge" at the Falls of the Schuylkill, Philadelphia, Pennsylvania (1808) Courtesy of Wikimedia Commons*

In 1801, not forty miles from Pittsburgh, from the vista of the banks of Jacob's Creek, Judge James Finley had a vision. His vision was the construction of a bridge over the small mountain stream, formed by a hanging chain, a chain whose *"height [was] suited to [its] breadth, [and its] breadth suited to [its] length..."* Born in Ireland, he immigrated to the US, became the owner of a 287-acre farm in Fayette County, Pennsylvania, was elected a justice of the peace in 1784, was elected County Commissioner in 1789, was then elected a member of the Pennsylvania House of Representatives and Senate, and finally from 1791 until his death, was an Associate Judge for Fayette County. His particular insight into mechanics and beauty took the form in the design, construction and patenting of the Jacob's Creek Bridge, a 70-foot span with the deck supported from a hanging chain, draped over pyramid styled piers. This modest but significant landmark, in engineering history, spanned a small stream immediately south of Mt. Pleasant, Pennsylvania – where the area adjacent to the site of the bridge still retains the name Iron Bridge in honor of Finley's accomplishment.

*The 1910 chain bridge at Newburyport, Massachusetts, replacing its 1810 predecessor in style and grace. Note the pyramid styled piers – a nod to Judge James Finely patented design. Photo courtesy of the Library of Congress.*

With his patent in hand, Finley produced over forty chain suspension bridges, including one at nearby Dunlap's Creek (The National Road), the Chain Bridge at Falls of Schuylkill, bridges over both the Potomac and Lehigh Rivers, and the Essex-Merrimac Bridge also known as the Newburyport (Massachusetts) Chain Bridge. Although none of these original Finley chain suspension bridges remain, the Newburyport Chain Bridge was noted by *Scientific American* in 1896 as "the solitary specimen in New England of a style of suspension bridge that has served its intentions admirably, and may still be found preferable to the wire bridges under certain circumstances." In 1910, a "replica" of Finely's patented design was constructed over the Merrimac River at the original Newburyport bridge site, a present and lasting reminder of America's first suspension bridge.

In the US, the suspension form of *harmonious rhythm of beauty and fitness* was improved and perfected by engineers of note including Amman, Ellet, Roebling, Steinman, Straus and many others. Throughout the world, record breaking suspension spans have been achieved in Japan, China, Denmark, Turkey, South Korea, United Kingdom, Norway and the US.

Cable-stayed bridge by the Renaissance polymath Fausto Veranzio, from 1595/1616. Courtesy of Wikimedia Commons

Even before Judge Finley had his inspiration, support of bridges from inclined cables were imagined by the visionaries of the Renaissance. In 1595, inventor Fausto Veranzio published his imaginative solution for a cable supported bridge with inclined stay cables in his book, *Machinae Novae*. However, the underlying physical principles of support were not clearly understood until Robert Hooke published his observation in 1676, by means of Latin anagram, familiar to many college engineering students: *"ut tensio, sic vis"* – i.e. "as the extension, so the force" – a fundamental, yet essential, expression of the linear elastic behavior of an idealized material – and in the case of Hooke, a watch spring.

A little more than 15 years after Finley's patent, a small Scottish footbridge, connecting the villages of Dryburgh and St. Boswells, spanning the River Tweed (namesake to the style of clothing), was erected with support based on a stayed cable principle. The Dryburgh Abbey Bridge, as it was known, had a very short life, and with only minimal success of several cable stayed designs in the early 1800s, the structural form was abandoned for some time. Roebling, reintroduced the concept, in connection with his suspension bridge designs, employing stayed cables to some success with his rehabilitation of the Wheeling Suspension Bridge (which was damaged in in a wind event), his Niagara Falls Suspension Bridge and his signature and final structure, the Brooklyn Bridge.

*The signature Millau Viaduct spanning the Tarn River Valley, in southern France, architecturally captures the essence of Vitruvius - harmonious rhythm of beauty and fitness. Photo courtesy of the author.*

With European pioneers like Dischinger, Morandi, de Miranda and Leonhardt, the modern cable-stayed bridge developed quickly in the post Second World War years. Starting with a single cable, or mono design, other and interesting forms of cable arrangements, with *harmonious rhythm of beauty and fitness,* including fanned, harped and star patterns, emerged. Throughout the world, record breaking suspension spans have been achieved in China, Russia, Japan, France, South Korea and Greece.

# *In the Shadow of the Brooklyn Bridge*
# *- David Steinman*

*"... around the (Brooklyn) bridge in afterglow, the city's lights like fireflies gleam ..." – poetry by David Steinman (Photo courtesy of the Library of Congress)*

*Against the city's gleaming spires,*
*Above the ships that ply the stream,*
*A bridge of haunting beauty stands –*
*Fulfillment of an artist's dream.*

The evocative twilight image of the Brooklyn Bridge and its – *"haunting beauty"* - came not from the heart of a poet but the soul of a Civil Engineer – David Steinman. Born in the late 1880s, and living in lower Manhattan as a youth, he literally grew up *in the shadow* of the Brooklyn Bridge. And by gazing at the silhouette of the Brooklyn Bridge and watching the construction of the nearby Williamsburg Bridge, he became, from a young age, captivated with bridges. This allure led to multiple degrees and teaching assignments in Civil Engineering.

*From deep beneath the tidal flow*
*Two granite towers proudly rise*
*To hold the pendent span aloft –*
*A harp against the sunset skies.*

As a young engineer, one can only hope to learn how to hold – *"a pendent span aloft"* - from the best. And Steinman did learn *from the best*, taking the role of special assistant to Gustav Lindenthal with the design of the Hell Gate Bridge, the iconic East River, New York City railroad crossing, with its expressive and powerful steel arched, through truss, linking Astoria and Wards Island. Steinman, along with Lindentahl and another of his protégés, Othmar Amman, became the trifecta of notable bridge forte in New York City in the early decades of the twentieth century.

*Each pylon frames, between its shafts,*
*Twin Gothic portals pierced with blue,*
*And crowned with magic laced design*
*Of lines and curves that Euclid knew.*

In the 1920's, Steinman joined forces with Holton Robinson and began a partnership in bridge design that lasted into the years of the Second World War. This venture emphasized economic designs over architecturally ornamented representations, yet never the less, produced some of America's most iconic suspension bridge designs – *"of the lines and curves that Euclid knew"* - including the Mount Hope Bridge spanning one of the narrowest gaps in the Narragansett Bay in Rhode Island, the St. John's Bridge spanning the Willamette River in Portland, Oregon, the Waldo-Hancock Bridge spanning the Penobscot River below Bangor, Maine, and the Deer Isle Bridge spanning Eggemoggin Reach, allowing vehicular passage from the Maine mainland to Little Deer Isle.

*The silver strands that form the net*
*Are beaded with the stars of night,*
*Lie jewelled dewdrops that adorn*
*A spiderweb in morning light.*

One of Steinman's greatest legacies is his *tour de force* book entitled *A Practical Treatise on Suspension Bridges, Their Design, Construction and Erection.* As Steinman states in his introduction, this book "… has been planned to supply the needs of practicing engineers who may have problems in estimating, designing and constructing suspension bridges … a practical handbook … distinguished by simplicity of treatment and convenience of application …" This 1922, John Wiley Book, now available on-line as a *Google Book*, not only explains how to evaluate the - *"spiderweb"* - which is useful even in the day of high speed computation, but also provides a historical treasure trove which is readily available to the bridge engineering historian. This work contains photographs and detail drawings of many long-forgotten legacy suspension bridges of an earlier generation, including the 1877 iconic, iron chain, Point (Suspension) Bridge spanning the Monongahela River in Pittsburgh, Lindenthal's 1884 braced chain Seventh Street Bridge in Pittsburgh, and, as proposed in 1921, but never realized, Lindenthal's life-long dream bridge – the 16 lane wide, braced chain, 57th Street Hudson River Crossing, simply known as the proposed Hudson River Bridge, traversing the Hudson from New Jersey to Manhattan, New York.

*Between the towers reaching high*
*A cradle for the stars is swung;*
*And from this soaring cable curve*
*A latticework of steel is hung.*

In 1884, a store owner in the small town of St. Ignace, at the southern tip of the upper peninsula of Michigan, published a newspaper advertisement that included a reprint of an artist's conception of the Brooklyn Bridge with the caption "Proposed Bridge Across the Straits of Mackinac". Seventy-three years later, the upper and lower peninsulas of Michigan were connected by – *"soaring cable curve(s)"*. Steinman's Mackinac Bridge, became known, in 1957 at its opening and still to this day, as the Western Hemisphere's longest suspension bridge (with two towers) between anchorages. As Steinman's most notable of designs, the bridge incorporated deep stiffening trusses – *"a latticework of steel"* – and an open-grid roadway to reduce wind resistance based on his

1943 published theoretical analysis of suspension-bridge stability problems, in response to the 1940 wind induced failure of the first Tacoma Narrows Bridge.

*Around the bridge in afterglow,*
*The city's lights like fireflies' gleam.*
*And eyes look up to see the span –*
*A poem stretched across the stream.*

from **BROOKLYN BRIDGE: NIGHTFALL, by** D. B. Steinman

From one who grew up *in the shadow* of the Brooklyn Bridge, the impression of the bridge, especially when night falls and the bridge lies in – *"afterglow"*, always stayed with Steinman. In 1945, he published a fond retelling of the bridge's story in a book entitled *The Builders of the Bridge: The Story of John Roebling and His Son;* and in 1948, he was commissioned to conduct a major rehabilitation of his favorite bridge - the Brooklyn Bridge.

*View from the Promenade looking towards Manhattan with Brooklyn Tower in the background.*
*Photo Courtesy of the Library of Congress*

# The Signature Bridges of David Steinman

" *... of lines and curves that Euclid knew ...* " *David Steinman – bridge designer, author and poet*

The 1931 **St. Johns Bridge** is a steel suspension bridge that spans the Willamette River in Portland Oregon, connecting the Cathedral Park neighborhood and the northwest industrial area. The bridge's two distinctive 408-foot-tall Gothic Towers gave the namesake to the adjacent park and neighborhood. On its June 13, 1931 dedication ceremony, David Steinman said: "*... A challenge and an opportunity to create a structure of enduring beauty in the God-given wondrous background was offered us when were asked to design the bridge. It is the most beautiful bridge in the world we feel ...*"

Photo Courtesy of the Library of Congress

The 1931 **Waldo–Hancock Bridge** (connecting Waldo and Handcock Counties) was the first long-span suspension bridge erected in Maine, as well as the first permanent bridge across the Penobscot River. The iconic bridge, with a main span of 800 feet was demolished in 2013. Technologically, the Waldo–Hancock Bridge represented a number of firsts. It was one of the first two bridges in the U.S. to employ Robinson and Steinman's prestressed twisted wire strand cables, and was also the first bridge to make use of the Vierendeel truss in its two towers, giving the structure an effect that Steinman called "artistic, emphasizing horizontal and vertical lines."

*Photo Courtesy of the Library of Congress*

The 1939 **Deer Isle Bridge** is a suspension bridge spanning Eggemoggin Reach in the state of Maine. The bridge, carrying State Route 15, is the only vehicular connection from the Maine mainland to Little Deer Island. With a main span of 1,088 feet, the bridge spanned the yachting area of the Eggemoggin Reach requiring a 200-foot wide channel at midspan with a minimum 85-foot underclearance, placing the roadway 100 feet above mean sear level, ultimately giving the structure a unique profile with steep (6.5%) approach grades and short (400 foot) vertical curve at mid-span.

Photo Courtesy of the Library of Congress

The 1957 **Mackinac Bridge** is the well-known suspension bridge spanning the Straits of Mackinac, connecting the Upper and Lower Peninsulas of Michigan. With an overall length of 26,372 feet, the "Mighty Mac" is the western hemisphere's longest suspension bridge between anchorages. At the time of construction, the bridge was noted for its deep stiffening deck truss and open grid deck with consideration of aerodynamic stability in an area noted for high winds. The bridge is also noted for its annual *Labor Day Bridge Walk*, where the bridge is closed to vehicular traffic and thousands of people, traditionally led by the Governor of Michigan, cross the five-mile span on foot from St. Ignace (upper or northern peninsula) to Mackinaw City (lower or southern peninsula).

Photo Courtesy of the Library of Congress

# CHAPTER 4

# THE ARCH

*arch* - a curved symmetrical structure spanning an opening and supporting the weight above it

*"An arch consists of two weaknesses which, leaning one against the other, make a strength." - Leonardo da Vinci*

# The Arch

*Île de la Cité*                                         *Right Bank of the Seine River*

*Le Pont Neuf*

*The New Bridge*
*Seine River*
*Paris, France*

*Construction Began -1578*
*Construction Completed – 1607*

*Le Pont Neuf is the oldest standing bridge across the Seine River in Paris France. The island to the left of the photo (Île de la Cité) is the birthplace of Paris, France, inhabited continuously from 225 BCE to the present.*

*Photos courtesy of the author.*

# The Arch - At the Intersection of Mathematics and Beauty

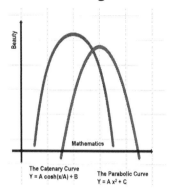

*Does any other fragment present a feat of structural engineering with such seemingly effortless grace? Leah Sinclair, 2014*

Who is not inspired by the form of the arch – be it created by nature or constructed by man? Who has not asked the question: How does such a slender form defy gravity and support such enormous weight with *effortless grace*? Throughout history, the arch has served two purposes – the first being to efficiently span a large distance – and the second being to reflect a monumental form of repetition and delight. While the origin of the arch is uncertain, many ancient cultures utilized its form, from the Mesopotamians constructing the simplest of structures, to the Chinese celebrating beauty and form, to the Romans celebrating victories and constructing large scale civilian works, to the medieval masons supporting their inspiring Gothic masterworks, and to our present bridge community combining efficiency and beauty in structural engineering. The arch's seductive form transcends time and cultures and has led to many of nature and man's most awe-inspiring creations.

But just what is an arch – is it as da Vinci said: *"... two weaknesses which, leaning against the other, make a strength?"* What defines its shape? Is it a simple mathematical statement or does it involve mathematics of complexity? What accounts for its beauty?

## The Catenary

*"I have lately received from Italy a treatise on the equilibrium of arches, by the Abbé Mascheroni. It appears to be a very scientific work. I have not yet had time to engage in it; but I find that the conclusions of his demonstrations are, that every part of the catenary is in perfect equilibrium. It is a great point in a new experiment, to adopt the sole arch, where the pressure will be borne by every part of it." from a letter written by Thomas Jefferson to Thomas Paine, on December 23, 1788 from Pairs France.*

Not realizing it at the time, Thomas Jefferson coined the term "catenary" – the true mathematical expression for the shape of an arch, which bears its own weight so efficiently that each element, along a line perpendicular to its axis, lies in uniform compression. While scant archeological evidence points to the Mesopotamians, who used a brick arch in rudimentary form some 4000 years ago, it was not until the advent of calculus that a secret of nature was revealed. The secret: the true shape of the most efficient structural form to support self-weight is the hyperbolic cosine – the catenary or a mathematical curve based on the natural exponential function ($e^x$).

*The Delicate Arch, Arches National Park, Utah*
*Photo is provided Courtesy of the National Park Service*

Nature itself abounds with evidence of this solution, as a trip to several of the National Parks in the US west will attest. Artisans of the Renaissance through modern times with no formal mathematical understanding but with a strong empirical sense of order, recognized that the inverse of a draped chain provided the exact blue print for the "true" shape of an arch. These artisans used this technique to perfection to construct such magnificent structures as the ceiling of the King's College Chapel, Cambridge, UK (built over a period of a hundred years from 1446–1531).

## The Semi-Circular Arch & the Romans

*"Architecture depends on Order ... Order gives due measure to the members of a work considered separately, and symmetrical agreement to the proportions of the whole ... There is also a kind of powder which from natural causes produces astonishing results. It is found ... in the country belonging to the towns round about Mt. Vesuvius. This substance, when mixed with lime and rubble, not only lends strength to buildings of other kinds ... let the masonry [of the aqueduct] be as solid as possible, and... let the masonry structure be arched over, so that the sun may not strike the water at all ...",* Ten Books on Architecture by Vitruvius, Books I, II & VII, c. 30 BCE.

*Roman bridge of Córdoba over the Guadalquivir River, a first century Roman bridge, rebuilt by the Moors in the 8th century and rehabilitated in 2006. Photo Courtesy of Jim Dwyer.*

The earliest surviving book on Roman architecture (by Vitruvius dedicated to his patron, Caesar Augustus) outlined the fundamentals of Roman thought and discovery which resulted ultimately in significant and long lasting monumental arched structures. What we may call structural engineering was viewed by the Romans as a combination of architecture and construction, founded on the mathematics of repeated, symmetrical, orderly geometric forms, the application of simple construction principles, and reliance on an abundant supply of raw materials and a cheap labor force. From the Roman point of view, an arch structure of any size would "work" as long as the proportions were appropriately scaled. In addition, the important discovery of manufactured cement, supplied by an abundance of nearby naturally occurring materials, facilitated the vision that any arch structure, be it a bridge, viaduct or aqueduct, of any size could be constructed. For the past 2,000 years, architecture has been inspired by this classical tradition. The resulting construction of arched masonry structures for bridges has followed the Roman model.

*Little Crossing Bridge, National Road (US 40) spanning the Casselman River Casselman State Park, Grantsville, MD. - Photo Courtesy of Author*

*[We have constructed] "the largest and we think the most permanent stone arch in the United States." November 16, 1814, HAER (Historical Architectural and Engineering Record).*

## *The Parabolic Arch*

By the early 1800's, materials with high strength to weight ratios began to systematically replace masonry as a backbone structure support. Examples included the "reinforcing" of the trussed elements of covered bridges with wooden arches to eliminate observable deflections. The construction tradesman at the time did not realize the basic physics of their construction: the arches were not simply "reinforcements" but were *the* principal load carrying members of the structural system. With advances in the understanding of engineering mechanics and new and exciting construction materials available in the 19th century, the weight of the arch, then constructed with cast iron, wrought iron and steel, became a very minor contributor to its load carrying capacity. A new structural form was needed. The new form, the parabola, is a pattern that repeats itself many times over in nature. Consider a wind-swept sand dune that experiences strong unidirectional winds. The resulting landscape reveals multiple ridges of arcing, parabolically profiled, dunes. Similarly, when the weight of the structure and live loads are principally equal and unidirectional, the parabola, with its noticeably sharply curved apex, becomes the most structurally efficient form to convey load. To reinterpret the 1788 observation of Thomas Jefferson: *"... every part of the [parabola] is in perfect equilibrium."*

Perhaps the parabola has become the most appealing architectural form. Why is this? Is it because the parabola is the shape of a projectile in motion, the spray of a garden hose or the path of a waterfall? Is it because of its mirror-imaged shape and its uniformly varying profile with distance? Is it because, when positioned at the focal point, directional light and sound waves are amplified? It is the beauty of the symmetry of the double image when an arch is reflected on a calm water surface? It is because when an arch is viewed at one position, it is symmetrical and logical and when viewed at another position, it becomes complex and undefinable?

Perhaps Frank Lloyd Wright, the father of organic architecture, and considered by some the "best American architect of all time", said it best:

*"I'll bridge these hills with graceful arches."* Frank Lloyd Wright.

*Vialduct over the Alamonte River, Caceres, Spain*

# Natural and Man-Made Arches
## A Little Quiz - some familiar arch bridges

Can you name this natural bridge and its location in this stunning landscape?

Can you name this man-made bridge and its location?

Can you name this natural bridge and its location in this stunning landscape?

Can you name this man-made bridge and its location?

Can you name this man-made bridge and its location in this stunning landscape?

Can you name this man-made bridge and its location?

## *BRIDGE QUIZ ANSWERS:*

1: The Devil's Bridge – Sedona, Arizona

2: The Rainbow Bridge – Niagara River, downstream of the falls, Niagara Falls, New York/Ontario Canada

3: Natural Bridge – Bryce Canyon , Utah

4: Pont Alexander III over the Seine River – Paris, France

5: Bixby Bridge – Big Sur, California

6. River Liffey (Ha'penny) Bridge – Dublin, Ireland

# Some not-so familliar arch bridges

The arch bridge, one of the oldest bridge types, has morphed over centuries from small stone and wooden bridges to large and graceful structures made of concrete and steel. Constructed all over the world by many different cultures, these bridges combine efficiency with aesthetics. The beauty of the arch type bridge - both natural and man-made - is certainly captured on the following few pages ... The quotations are a composite of the observations of many bridge enthusiasts.

*Bridge of Sighs over the River Cam, Cambridge, UK*
*"Great composition and colors!... Charming setting!... Reflects the history of the arch bridge!"*

This beautiful Neo-Gothic covered bridge crosses the River Cam on the campus of St. John's College Cambridge. The bridge was built in 1831 to connect the original campus to new structures built on the west side of the river to accommodate the increasing student population. The bridge has very little in common with it's namesake in Venice, Italy other than it is covered. The Venetian bridge led to a prison and provided convicts with their last view of Venice resulting in many "sighs". Rumor has it, students named this Cambridge bridge similarly as many pre-exam students were heard "sighing" as they crossed the bridge from their rooms heading to exams in buildings on the east side of the river.

CSX A-Line Bridge over the James River, Richmond, VA
"Fantastic contrast ... Great composition ... Surreal reality"

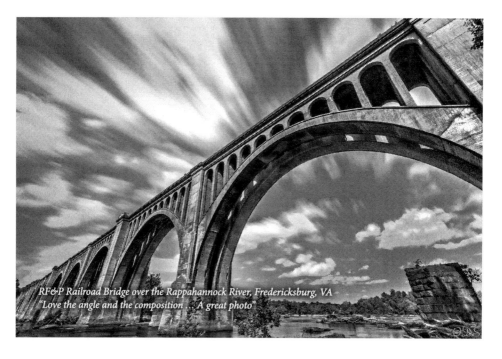

RF&P Railroad Bridge over the Rappahannock River, Fredericksburg, VA
"Love the angle and the composition ... A great photo"

*Croton Reservoir Dam Bridge over the Croton River, Croton Gorge Park, Croton-on-Hudson, NY*
*"Wonderful capture of light ... you can almost hear the roaring Croton River"*

*Yaquina Bay Bridge, Newport, Oregon*
*"Composition and subject matter are wonderful ... Very cohesive photo"*

Gapstow Bridge over the Pond, Central Park, New York City, New York
"Good color contrast ... Striking contrast between the urban city and the park"

Mike O'Callaghan-Pat Tillman Memorial Bridge over the Colorado River, Arizona/Nevada Border
"Lots of drama ... Excellent composition"

*Norfolk Southern RR Bridge over the Susquehanna River, Harrisburg, Pennsylvania*
*"Peacefulness … Colors and content are striking"*

*Owachomo Bridge, Arches National Park, Utah*
*"Such interesting scenery … One can never cease to be amazed at nature's wonders"*

Double Arch Natural Bridge, Arches National Park, Utah
"Interesting image ... Dramatic ... Enormity of scale is evidenced by the human reference points"

"Nature is pleased with simplicity. And nature is no dummy" - Isaac Newton

# Arch Bridges & Pittsburgh's Greatest Bridge Decade

*"Works great in one age of the profession will be superseded by greater experience of future times" John B. Jervis, 1869*

## A Snapshot in Time

The ten-year period from 1924 to 1934 was the ***greatest bridge decade*** in the City of Pittsburgh and Allegheny County.[1] There has never been or will their likely ever be, another ten-year period that sees such monumental bridge construction in either the City of Pittsburgh or Allegheny County. Within the ***greatest bridge decade***, eight new bridges were constructed over the three rivers within one mile of the point. In that same time period, many other bridges, both large and small, were constructed over the rivers and valleys of Allegheny County.

The *"... greater experience of future times ..."* was at hand with the completion (in 1932) of the West End Bridge and the George Westinghouse Bridge, both majestic and iconic arch bridges.

> *"There are two main divisions of city planning. One look to the rearrangement and improvement of what has already been unwisely done ... the other looks to the wise and economical layout of what still remains to be done ..." Frederick Law Olmstead, Jr. (world famous landscape architect and son of creator of New York's Central Park) in his Report to the (Pittsburgh) City Planning Commission, 1911.*

"... in the early 20th century, planners such as ... Olmstead, Jr. ... merged park planning and civic art towards a truly comprehensive vison of the organic city ..." John Banmen, 2006.

---

[1] Pittsburgh is the county seat and economic engine of Allegheny County, Pennsylvania

## *The year is 1932*

Two marvelous arch bridges have been completed in the Pittsburgh Region.

The design and construction of these architecturally marvelous bridges was over twenty years in the making. The forces that came to bear were a combination of social, political and environmental. Consider:

- **1911** Frederick Law Olmstead, Jr.'s seminal urban planning study for Pittsburgh, *Report 8,* entitled *Pittsburgh, Main Thoroughfares and the Downtown District, Improvements Necessary to Meet the City's Present and Future Needs,* was finalized and presented to the City Planning Commission.

- In his report, Olmstead, Jr., (a leading American landscape architect of the early 20th century and son of the famous landscape architect of New York's Central Park) wryly noted that "… Considering that fact that Pittsburgh is a world capital in the steel bridge industry, that its busiest quarters are sundered by three of the worlds big rivers, … it is a striking and rather shameful thing that it does not possess a single bridge over its rivers that is notable among the bridges of the world either for its beauty, for its perfect engineering adaptation to its purpose, for its size, strength or amplitude. In fact, the bridges of Pittsburgh, compared with those of other great cities are rather unusually limited in capacity and lacking in the qualities of impressiveness and beauty."

- **1918** Allegheny County created its own Planning Commission. Over time an intense rivalry developed between the City and County planning commissions as they vied for public money and bonds to finance projects.

- **1924** The Allegheny County Department of Public Works and County Commissions orchestrated a campaign of public support which resulted in the passing of a significant bond measure that funded Allegheny County public works project for the next decade. The County's bond measure funded the construction of all major highway river crossings over all three rivers near the point from 1924 to 1934.

- **1925** Allegheny County, Department of Public Works, with the assistance of Frederick Bigger, developed a *Major Highway Plan*, described as the "Ultimate Highway System" consisting of a web-like system of radial and ring roads (presently the color-coded belt designations), centered about downtown Pittsburgh.

With the passage of the 1924 bond measure, and adoption of the 1925 *Major Highway Plan*, Allegheny County looked to implement that part of the plan which would provide boulevard access through the principal river valleys of the region and would move traffic to and from the city and by-passing Pittsburgh at key points.

Ultimately the West End Bridge and George Westinghouse Bridge can be viewed as important but small components of much larger transportation improvement projects. As with the Liberty Bridge and Tunnels, bridges were no longer a just means to convey traffic from one shore to another, but were parts of a much larger and well-orchestrated transportation network. The West End Bridge and its connecting roadway through the Saw Mill Run Valley, as well as the George Westinghouse Bridge, high above the Turtle Creek Valley, and its connection to Ardmore Boulevard, embraced the principles of professional planning sought for in the 1925 *Major Highway Plan*.

## The year is 1933

In 1933 the Neal Deal began with emergency legislation enacted to end the depression. This legislation included the National Recovery Administration, Agricultural Adjustment Act, Federal Emergency Relief, and Works Progress Administration. Pittsburgh anxiously awaited federal money for public works. Little money materialized. With the completion of the West End Bridge and George Westinghouse Bridge in 1932, the era of major bridge construction in Pittsburgh near the point was over and would not return until Pittsburgh's Renaissance and the Interstate Era, in the late 1950's.

*Other notable bridges constructed in the City of Pittsburgh and Allegheny County in the **greatest bridge decade** – 1924 -1934 - include:*

1924 – Fortieth Street Bridge (Washington's Crossing) – steel plate girder arch over the Allegheny River.

1927 – Second Point Bridge – Steel Cantilever Truss.

1926-1928 – the iconic Three Sister Bridges over the Allegheny River – self-anchored suspension bridges, each with 430-foot main spans.

1928 – Thirty-First Street Bridge – steel plate girder arch over the Allegheny River.

1930 – East Street Bridge – large steel cantilever truss, 225 feet above the floor of the East Street Valley.

1931 – McKees Rocks bridge over the Ohio River – steel trussed arch with a 750-foot main span.

1933 – South Tenth Street Bridge over the Monongahela River – steel suspension bridge with a725-foot main span

*West End Bridge, West Approach - October 1931*
*Photo Courtesy of the Allegheny County, Department of Public Works*

*Pittsburgh Fact: In 1832, a salt processing facility – i.e. salt works - lay along and over Saw Mill Run at its confluence with the Ohio River, at approximately the same location that the west approach to the West End Bridge lies today (from a painting by Russell Smith). – The small culvert in foreground (of the photo of the preceding page) is Saw Mill Run and the Site of 1832 "salt works".*

Construction Photo Courtesy of the Allegheny County, Department of Public Works
*The tied arch is a delicate structure. Until the arch was closed the structural form was unstable and an intricate system of temporary support in the Ohio River was required.*

George Westinghouse Bridge
*Perhaps, the Pittsburgh Region's and Allegheny County's most iconic bridge constructed in the **greatest bridge decade.***
Photo Courtesy of the Library of Congress

*Pittsburgh Fact: If you are standing on the deck of the George Westinghouse Bridge, 240 feet above the Turtle Creek Valley, and are gazing west, you will see the Monongahela River (9 miles upstream from the point) and Braddock, PA - the site of Braddock's Defeat in 1755 and later the site of the Andrew Carnegie's first steel mill in the Pittsburgh region – the Edgar Thomson Works.*

## *Bridge Footnote:*

The Westinghouse Bridge is a fixed, concrete arch bridge – the foundations resist the outward thrust (or push) of the arches.

The West End Bridge is a steel, tied-arch bridge – the slender steel deck superstructure girders (the "tie") resist the thrust of the main span arch.

# CHAPTER 5

# WATER CROSSINGS

*river* - a large natural stream of water flowing in a channel to the sea

*bay* - a broad inlet of the sea where the land curves inward

*"We had a succession of black nights, going up the river, and it was observable that whenever we landed ... a certain curious effect was always produced: hundreds of birds flocked instantly out from the masses of shining green foliage ... and often a song-bird tuned up and fell to singing."*
*- Mark Twain, Life on the Mississippi*

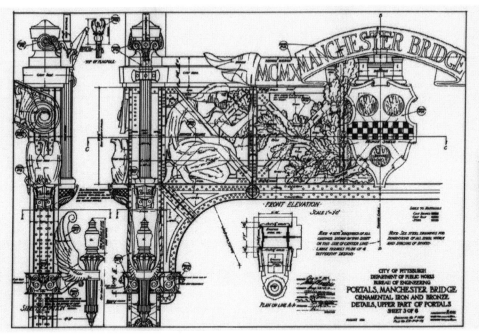

# Water Crossings

*Manchester Bridge Portal memorializing explorer Christopher Gist travels in 1753 to Pittsburgh (as a guide to George Washington en route to challenge French expansion to the Ohio River)*

*The Artwork on the Bridge was a direct result of the empowerment of the Pittsburgh Art Commission, chartered to oversee the "City Beautification", based on the recommendation of Frederick Law Olmstead, Jr.'s seminal master planning study report to the city entitled Pittsburgh, Main Thoroughfares and the Downtown District, dated 1911.*

*Images courtesy of the Library of Congress*

*Manchester Bridge, spanning the Allegheny River, near the confluence of the Allegheny and Monongahela Rivers, City of Pittsburgh, 1910-1971*

# Perfection and Beauty Unsurpassable - the Eads Bridge

*"...I have haunted the river every night lately, where I could get a good look at the bridge by moonlight. It is indeed a structure of perfection and beauty unsurpassable, and I never tire of it."*

Walt Whitman, 1879 - American poet extraordinaire and brother of an Eads bridge laborer. When Whitman penned these words, the bridge (over the Mississippi River at St. Louis, Missouri) was only five years old, but had already become a world-wide symbol of America's genius and promise.

To the poet, the layman and the engineer, from 1874 to the present, the Eads Bridge captivates the imagination. It has been symbol of daring and beauty from its first construction. As the first symbol for the city of St. Louis as the gateway to the west, it was transfixed into an iconic manifestation with the creation of the St. Louis arch in 1965. What was it that has generated such appeal – an appeal to engineers and artists alike?

*"Must we admit that because a thing never has been done, it never can be?"*
*- James B. Eads*

In 1797, Captain James Piggott piloted the first ferry across the Mississippi River at St. Louis. Bold plans for a Mississippi River crossing were proposed first in 1839 by Charles Ellet (the father of suspension bridges) who envisioned a 900-1200-900 ft suspension span for pedestrians and carriages, again in 1855 by Josiah Dent who suggested a rail road suspension bridge and once again a year later by Roebling who also envisioned a suspension bridge. And then the civil war intervened.

Enter James Buchannan Eads, hydraulic engineer and a civil war captain who, in1861, at the call of the Federal government, constructed ironclad steamers, gunboats and mortar boats, all of use in opening up the Mississippi and its tributaries throughout the Civil War. In 1879, he designed his last major hydraulic work, a system of willow mattresses and stonework at the mouth of the Mississippi River, where the water was confined to a narrow passage through which the river scoured a deep channel to permit the passage of boats. In 1867 Eads proposed a daring river crossing at St. Louis, Missouri. Eads was armed with the knowledge, borne of his river experience, that in the Mississippi River, the largest threat is scour and if scour could be eliminated, a wonderful work could be accomplished. Having been abroad before the war studying European public works such as the Koblenz Bridge, it no surprise that he envisioned a structure based on a classical style. This style would emphasize imposing pier elements of stone, which would gain their needed support from bedrock, as much as 100 feet below the low water of the Mississippi. The stone pier elements would then be connected by a repetitive and structurally efficient superstructure form.

*"[Trussed arches were a] ... form which often combines the highest economy with the most elegant and graceful proportions in architecture"* - James B. Eads

*Eads Bridge over the Mississippi River, St. Louis Missouri*
*Photo Courtesy of the Library of Congress*

The true grace of the Eads Bridge is the interplay of strength and delicacy. Strength was achieved though the massive stone river piers and classically styled approach spans balanced by delicacy, which was achieved through the wispy yet handsome superstructure, comprising a series of flat parabolic arches spanning a record (at the time of) 500 feet, each. The arches were trussed in vertical pairs with four pairs per span, intricately braced with interconnecting diagonal elements. Over objections to the fabricators of the era, the arches were formed from hollow steel tubes, with exacting and demanding metallurgical specification requirements. The result was a marriage of form and function, the grace of a classical architectural form coupled with the efficiency of the parabolic pressure line directing forces into slender tubes, of almost ethereal shape.

In essence, this bridge is visually appealing by applying the modernist creed of less being more. Eads decided to allow the essential beauty of stone and steel and form to carry the load without other aesthetic adornment.

> *"Here was romance, here was a man, the great adventurer daring to think, daring to have faith daring to do... [The] bridge was to cross a great river, to form the portals of a great city, to be sensational and architectonic." - Louis Sullivan, Chicago Architect, credited with the first modern steel skyscraper changing load resistance paradigm from bearing wall to the emerging skeletal support construction with an outer skin construction. Sullivan credited his inspiration from Eads and was the architect for one of St. Louis architectural treasures, the Wainwright Building at Seventh and Chestnut Streets.*

The bridge was completed in 1874; some notable (and not so notable) achievements with the design and construction include:

- First major bridge to cross the Mississippi River (between Illinois and Missouri, although there were a few upper river crossings previously built).

- Designed with capacity to convey both railroad traffic of the day as well as pedestrians and carriages (and presently carries transit and vehicular traffic).

- Originally named the Illinois & St. Louis Bridge, it was later named for its designer.

- First major bridge to make extensive use of steel alloy for the truss and bracing system (including innovations for precision and accuracy of construction and quality control, as well as utilization of cast chromium steel components).

- First major bridge with arch spans of 500 ft (longest span is 520 feet).

- First major bridge to use cantilevered construction, avoiding falsework that would hinder river traffic (bowing to the politically influential river industry).

- First major bridge in the U.S. to use the pneumatic caissons for deep underwater pier construction (which sadly led to considerable illness and some deaths from the "bends" – i.e. decompression sickness due to nitrogen in the bloodstream).

- Although an engineering and architectural success, the bridge owners (i.e. the St. Louis Bridge and Iron Company) went bankrupt within the first year of opening.

- Designated as a National Historic Landmark.

*"[Eads believed that]… the true, the useful, and the beautiful were equally manifest in the harmony of creation. Machines that worked right looked right because utility and taste were one in the mind of God." - Howard S. Miller, Missouri State Historian and co-author (with Quinta Scott) of the book, "The Eads Bridge".*

# *Postscript*

Besides James Buchannan Eads, some industry giants and other historical figures played important and sometimes interesting roles in the Eads Bridge including:

- Ead's Chief inspector was Theodore Cooper (a name well renowned in railroad design, and the name of historically and currently affixed to railroad design loadings).

- In 1869, Andrew Carnegie secured bonds from European investors for the construction of the bridge and was subsequently made a member of the board of directors for the bridge.

- William Tecumsch Sheman drove the last spike on June 9, 1874.

- John Robinson led a "test (circus) elephant" across the new Eads Bridge to prove it was safe. (It was believed at that time that elephants had instincts that would keep them from setting foot on unsafe structures.) The bridge was opened, with ceremony, on July 4, 1874.

- Jay Gould (railroad magnate) become the owner of the bridge in 1881 by coercion (as he persuaded Congress to grant a congressional charter for a "new" bridge 45 miles upstream, effectively lowering the selling price of the Eads Bridge; Gould had no intention of building a "new" bridge upstream).

*Tonight, I've inherited the soul of James B. Eads.*

*I am science, civil engineering,*

*That grand tributary, the Mississippi River,*

*The forces of nature tamed by this mathematics,*

*The colossal Eads Bridge Itself,*

*Spanning the rapid currents of my imagination.*

*From "The Soul of Eads" by Louis Daniel Brodsky, sometimes poet, businessman and proprietor of Time Being Books in St. Louis*

# The Eads Bridge –
# a Pittsburgh Connection

*"Those were the times when one man, alone, could create a bridge (Eads), or a tower (Gustave Eiffel) or an architectural school (Louis Sullivan)." - Howard S. Miller, Missouri State Historian and co-author (with Quinta Scott) of the book, The Eads Bridge.*

*"The Eads Bridge of St Louis is of special interest to the steel industry because it was not only the first bridge to make extensive use of steel, but was one of the first significant steel structures of any type." - John K Edmonds, American Institute of Steel Construction*

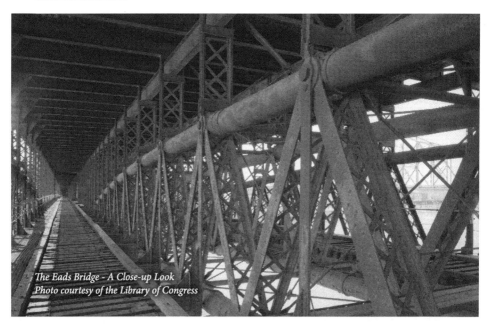

The Eads Bridge - A Close-up Look
Photo courtesy of the Library of Congress

One may not be aware, but the superstructure of the Eads Bridge and the city of Pittsburgh are deeply intertwined.

On April 9, 1865, the Civil War essentially ends with Lee's surrender to Grant at Appomattox Court House, Virginia. In that same year there were two very important milestones in the life of Andrew Carnegie and the construction of the Eads Bridge: (1) Andrew Carnegie "retires" from the railroad; and (2) with a loan of $80,000, Andrew Carnegie and several associates reorganize the Piper and Schiffler Company into the Keystone Bridge Company, as the investors envision building bridges of iron rather than wood. With headquarters in an office building at the corner of 6th Avenue and Grant Streets, downtown Pittsburgh, and their first mill, the Union Mills at 34th Street along the Allegheny River, Andrew Carnegie and his brother, Thomas Carnegie, began their careers in the iron (and eventually steel) industries.

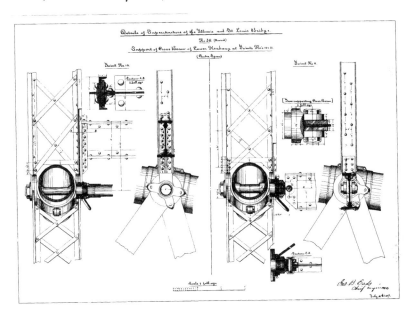

*Engineering Drawing: Details of the Superstructure of the Illinois and St. Louis Bridge (later named the Eads Bridge after its designer). This image is a copy is one of many original design drawings of the Eads Bridge transferred from The American Bridge Company Archives to the Washington University (St. Louis) in 1980. Note James Eads' signature on the drawing. Image is courtesy of Jim Dwyer.*

In 1870 the Union Iron Mills were reorganized under the name of the Isabella Furnace Company and a new blast furnace was built, seventeen blocks away, on 51st Street in the Lawrenceville Section of Pittsburgh. The blast furnace, named the Lucy furnace after Thomas Carnegie's wife, was enormous by the standards of the day, standing at 75 feet (23m) in height, and was producing 270 tons per day by 1872. During this time of remarkable tonnage, this furnace was producing all of the iron tonnage for the steel for the superstructure of the Eads

Bridge, which included the 100,000 psi structural barrel staves, which are the hollow tube steel members that uniquely characterize this bridge.

By 1900, Thomas Carnegie had died and Andrew Carnegie sold all steel interests, and the Keystone Bridge Company was one of 28 companies absorbed into the American Bridge Company along with a vast repository of engineering drawings. In 1980, a colleague of the author came in possession of a copy of an 1871 drawing signed by James Buckhannon Eads himself. The drawing (on the preceding page) displays the intricate bracing system nestled within the Eads Bridge's steel superstructure. Not only is the bridge an engineering marvel and aesthetic joy, but the engineering drawings of the day were masterpieces of drafted "art".

*The Eads Bridge, St. Louis MO, Photo courtesy of the Library of Congress*

# The Intersecting Legacies of Roebling & Cooper and the Allegheny River Crossing

There are many famous bridge luminaries of the nineteenth century. Among them are John Roebling, the noted engineer of the Brooklyn Bridge, and Theodore Cooper, who is best known for standardized railroad loading. Their legacies intersected in a unique way in Pittsburgh in the early 1890s.

> *"... the wire is in as good condition as new, ... the anchorages are so thoroughly protected that they are good for at least one hundred years ..." J. H. Hildebrand, 1888*

Joel Henry Hildebrand was employed to examine the cable and anchorages of John Roebling's, third and last Pittsburgh Bridge, the iconic Allegheny River Suspension Bridge, connecting the City of Allegheny (presently the North Side) with the downtown business district at the site of the present day Sixth Street Bridge. The graceful bridge was punctuated with cast iron towers with parabolic suspension cables and stay cables radiating from each of the towers. In 1888, Hildebrand foresaw a limitless future for this bridge with such beautiful and graceful lines.

Within two years, a quantum shift in technology took place – the electric street car came into use, and this beautiful, but light and flexible bridge crossing could not capably support the heavier vehicles, and its lifetime, a mere thirty years, came quickly to an end.

> *"... the Allegheny Suspension Bridge was long noted as the most beautiful and graceful in its lines ..." W. G. Wilkins, 1895, looking back in time.*

In 1890, electric street-cars came to Pittsburgh. Sixth Street (former St. Clair Street) was the main thoroughfare between the business districts of Pittsburgh and the City of Allegheny. Tracks were laid on the Roebling Suspension Bridge with unsatisfactory results. Horse drawn wagons, plodding across the bridge, were slowing down the "rapid transit" and vibrations and deflections from the electric street-cars were a concern. The bridge toll owners determined that a replacement bridge was necessary and devised a scheme to construct the new bridge around the suspension bridge so that both pedestrians and electric street-car traffic could continue without interruption.

Design for the new bridge was tasked to Theodore Cooper, a renowned bridge engineer, who had personally served as the chief inspector of construction on the Eads Bridge over the Mississippi River. Cooper proportioned an elegant bow string truss with a design based on his own "1890 Highway Bridge Specifications". His 'specifications', which prescribed design loadings and permissible unit strains (stresses), represented a leap forward in rational bridge design.

> " ... The most perfect system of rules to insure success must be interpreted upon the broad ground of professional intelligence and common sense ... " Theodore Cooper

Cooper designed a two-span simply supported, bowstring truss bridge to span the Allegheny. To meet the objective of maintaining continuous street-car traffic, the following novel construction approach was followed.

- The mid-stream river pier was aligned with the existing piers on the Union Bridge, at the Point, and Lindenthal's Seventh Street Bridge. Survey work, to determine a precise pier location of the pier, was conducted at 4:00 in the morning so as not to interfere with the street-cars.

- The stone river pier was built on a heavy timber grillage founded on a thick stratum of glacial gravel within the river bed – a common construction method of the day.

- Eight hundred piles were driven to erect a temporary wooden trestle extending across the entire width of the river (except for one small location to allow steamboat passage).

- The deck of the old suspension bridge was placed on blocks and fully supported by the timber trestle.

- Two additional wooded pile trestles were built on either side of the suspension bridge to support a large erection gantry which would hoist and temporarily support each new steel truss, each extending over 70 feet above the bridge deck at mid-span.

- The large erection gantries - taller than the highest point on the bowstring truss – erected the new, two span truss bridge, one span at a time. Remarkably, it only took 8 days to fully erect one complete truss span. The plan was successful – the total lost time to street-cars over the course of erection of the new bridge was three hours.

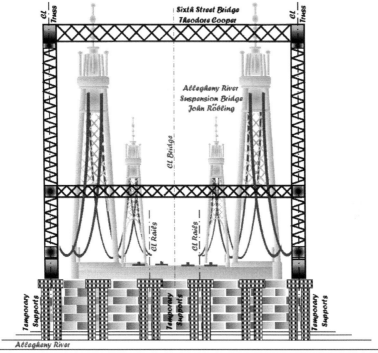

**Construction Illustration, c. 1891**

After Cooper's new bridge was opened to traffic, the old Allegheny Suspension Bridge, Roebling's third and last bridge treasure in Pittsburgh, was dismantled. Then the street-car tracks were raised to final elevation by hydraulic jacks and blocked into position.

The elegant bowstring truss remained a toll bridge until 1911 when the County of Allegheny obtained ownership. In 1927, the two bowstring truss spans were 'recycled' – to make way for a new river crossing. The truss spans were floated four miles downstream to a new home and became the bridge to Coraopolis over the back channel of the Ohio River.

Theodore Cooper developed and published the first *General Specifications for Iron Railroad Bridges and Viaducts* in 1884. *Engineering News Record*, a major industry publication, call it the "first authoritative specification on bridge construction that had been published and circulated." Cooper then published the *Specifications for Highway Bridges* in 1890, and reissued it with updates in 1896, 1901, and 1906.

These specifications were the basis of many more editions to come, leading up to present day bridge codes. Railroad bridge codes show Cooper's legacy best, as train loads are still referred to as "Cooper-E" loading with numeric designations for weight. When Theodore Cooper passed away in 1919, he had spent over 40 years as a bridge engineer. The obituary in the New York Times referred to him as a "Builder of Great Bridges".

Pittsburgh's 1892 6th Street Bridge over the Allegheny River was one of them.

*Allegheny River Suspension Bridge (1859)*
*Photo Courtesy of Carnegie Library*

*Bridge Design by John Roebling*

Allegheny River Suspension Bridge (1892)
Photo Courtest of Carnegie Library

Bridge Design by Theodore Cooper

6th Street Bridge - relocated to the back channel of the Ohio River at Coraopolis, PA (1927-1995)
Photo Courtesy of the Library of Congress

# BRIDGES of the Chesapeake
# The Rhythm of the Tides

Chesapeake is Tidewater; Tidewater is the Chesapeake. From the colony of Jamestown to the battle of the Monitor and the Merrimac, to the impressive ship yards of Norfolk, the inland waterway of the Chesapeake has been an important transportation node where shipping, rail and highway modes of transportation converge. On the one hand, Mother Nature has been kind to provide a large protected bay, some 3,230 square miles to be precise. On the other hand, Mother Nature has been cruel with her subsurface soils – sands, soft clays and shelly coquinas – leaving a challenge for the both the design and construction of bridges and their foundations – the base upon which the transportation modes must be constructed.

The bridges of the Chesapeake are fascinating. Their lengths are grand. Their construction challenges were many. To appreciate the utility of travel is to appreciate the visible superstructure. But to appreciate the visible superstructure, it is first necessary to understand the regional geology and appreciate the skills of the artisans that constructed the foundations as well as the superstructures of these monumental structures.

## From Beyond Earth's Orbit

In the mid-Cenozoic Era (35 Ma), a bolide from outer space impacted the earth's surface near Cape Charles, Virginia. Although not understood until the early 1990s, it is now evident by seismic surveys and deep sedimentary core interpretation that this large meteoritic fireball or possibly a comet, with a diameter greater than one mile, carved a 55 mile wide by 2,000 foot deep crater, the largest in the continental United States. This resulting deep basin became the outlet for the ancient Susquehanna River to the Atlantic Ocean. The effects of the crater have influenced sediment deposition; and even to the present, briny groundwater, associated with the crater, is a problem for many deep water wells in eastern Virginia. With a series of glacial advances and retreats, the ancient Susquehanna carved a route to the coast. At the height of the last glacial epoch, seal level dropped to 450 feet below its present level near Cape Henry. Rising waters from the melting glaciers of the Pleistocene age reached the mouth of the Chesapeake Bay about 10,000 years ago where sea level continued to rise, drowning a series of river beds, until the Bay as we know it today was formed about 3,000 years ago. With subsequent glacial retreat, the valleys were drowned and became relatively shallow bays and estuaries underlain by loads of deep sediment – sands, soft clays and shelly coquinas - forming the complex network of bay soils with depths extending to 450 feet near Capes Charles and Henry.

*Chesapeake Bay is a translation of the Powhatan Native American word "chesepiooc" which means "Great Shellfish Bays." At the time of the first European settlement, the tidewater area was inhabited by an estimated 13,000 to 14,000 Powhatan Native Americans. The first European to enter the Chesapeake Bay region was Spanish explorer Vicente Gonzalez in 1561. In 1605, the French started a colony at Port Royal (now Annapolis). In 1607, the Jamestown settlement was established on the James River. In 1634, Lord Baltimore, who had been granted the land from the Potomac River to the north by the King of England, established the first English colony in Maryland, known as St. Mary's City. The first light house built by the United States was built in 1792 at Cape Henry (named for Henry Frederick, Prince of Wales), marking the entrance to the Chesapeake Bay. (The north and opposite cape was named Cape Charles, for Henry Frederick's younger brother, Charles, the Duke of York.)*

# Crossing the James River Estuary

The first serious attempt to cross the Chesapeake with a fixed structure as documented in historic Civil War photos. This crossing of the James River Estuary, upstream from its mouth to the Chesapeake was a pontoon bridge constructed in the 1860s. Foundations were avoided; the bay was crossed.

The first fixed crossing of the Chesapeake Bay was a two lane bridge with lift span connecting Newport News on the Virginia Peninsula with Isle of Wight

County in the South Hampton Roads region. The privately-owned James River Bridge Corporation was chartered by the General Assembly to build a system of bridges across the James River, Chuckatuck Creek, and Nansemond River. The common foundation type in this geological setting at the time of construction was wooden pilings. These large displacement foundations with limited penetration resulted in clusters of pilings at each foundation, especially when a lift span was involved. When completed, the 4.5-mile bridge was the longest bridge in the world over water. The $5.2 million James River Bridge was opened on November 17, 1928 by the press of a button in Washington, D.C., where U.S. President Calvin Coolidge, sitting in the Oval Office of the White House, sent an electric signal to lower into place the upraised lift span over the James River channel.

*James River Crossing - c. 1938; Image Courtesy of Historic Hampton Roads*

The bridge, carrying US-17 was replaced with four-lane bridge and was completed in stages from 1975 to 1982. The 415 foot lift span of the replacement structure provides 145 feet of vertical clearance at high tide, a significant increase over the original bridge. Only a small portion of the original bridge remains in use today as a fishing pier.

## The Bay Bridge

The second significant fixed crossing of the Chesapeake Bay was an elevated structure constructed south of Annapolis, Maryland, connecting the Maryland peninsula to the mainland. In 1908, private investors in Baltimore advocated the first plans for a trolley bridge crossing the Chesapeake Bay near Baltimore, but the proposal was dismissed. In 1938, the Maryland State Roads Commission determined that the best site for a Chesapeake Bay bridge was between Sandy Point and Kent Island, a four mile link which would replace the ferry from Annapolis to Queen Anne's County, and would provide better service from the Annapolis-Baltimore-Washington "triangle" to the eastern shore. However, World War II intervened and there was no serious consideration for a crossing until hostilities ceased.

Ten years later, construction contracts for the 123 span Bay Bridge, carrying Route 50, were awarded. The bridge featured a sweeping curved alignment and a 1,600 foot main suspension span over the main channel. While the bay is relatively shallow at this location, pilings for the foundations were barged for considerable distances. Never the less the most serious challenge from nature were the high winds associated with the open waterway expanse. Consider that Between 1951 and 1960, Virginia was affected by 16 major storms; the most sever occurring in August of 1955, when Hurricane Connie moved up the Chesapeake Bay and across Baltimore and only five days later, Hurricane Diane moved across central Virginia, Richmond and Washington, D.C. Rain from the two storms set records for the month of August over central and northern Virginia.

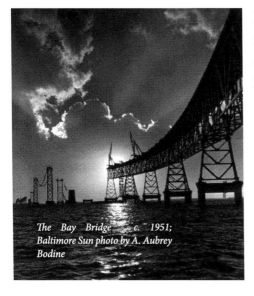

*The Bay Bridge c. 1951; Baltimore Sun photo by A. Aubrey Bodine*

By the close of 1950, the two 354-foot main towers, and the concrete anchorages that support the two main cables were completed, with the spinning of the two 14-inch-diameter main cables commencing in early 1951. To provide additional bracing against the frequent high winds on the bay, stiffening through trusses were placed above the roadway. The roadway sections of the main suspension span were hoisted into place during late 1951. By 1952 the bridge was opened to the public. In 1967, the state recommended that priority be given to a new bridge parallel to the existing crossing, leading some to call the bridge (most ironically, post Watergate) the "Agnew's Double-Cross" after the then-current governor, Spiro Agnew. At present the Bay Bridge carries approximately 65,000 vehicles per day on the average weekday; this number swells to as 95,000 vehicles per day on summer weekends.

## The Chesapeake Bay Bridge-Tunnel – at the mouth of the Chesapeake

Cape Charles Virginia, to the north and Cape Henry Virginia to the south were separated by the 17 mile mouth of the Chesapeake Bay – literally worlds apart until 1964, when Chesapeake Bay Bridge-Tunnel was opened to traffic. The 42 month construction period included construction of 12 miles of low-level trestle, two one-mile tunnels, four miles of bridges and four man-made islands.

By the early 1960s, very efficient foundation elements were available for complex construction projects in bay settings. The structure, carrying Route 13, is supported by 5,000 precast, prestressed concrete cylinder piles, 54 inches in outside diameter. These thin walled piles (with a 5 inch wall thickness) result in low displacement foundations with optimized penetration resulting in relatively few pile penetrations per substructure unit. The seabed materials entered the void in the center of the piles during pile driving. Piles were manufactured and transported 180 miles from the project site. From a floating barge and crane, the piles, ranging in length of 140 to 180 feet were driven from 80 feet to 150 feet into the bay soils of sands and soft clays. Not anticipated at the time of construction was the potential damage the driving hammer could inflict on the thin walled sections. The resulting hairline fracture zones became catalysts for salt water, chloride intrusion necessitating ultimately jacketed repairs with galvanic cathodic protection completed in 2009.

The 1960s construction was accomplished under the severe conditions imposed by nor'easters, hurricanes, and the unpredictable Atlantic Ocean. During the Ash Wednesday Storm of 1962, much of the work partially completed and the

*Chesapeake Bay Bridge-Tunnel, c. 1965; Photo courtesy of CBB-T*

custom-built $1.5-million Big D pile driver was destroyed. In 1965, one year after opening, the two lane facility was selected as one of the Seven Engineering Wonders of the Modern Works and as recently as 2002, Civil Engineering Magazine named it one of the Landmarks in Civil Engineering History. A parallel bridge-tunnel was completed in 1999 increasing the vehicular capacity to four lanes and serving over 3,500,000 vehicles per year.

## The View is Tremendous

As one travels down Route 13 from New England to Florida and one travels along the coast of the Delmarva Peninsula towards Virginia, the last water gap, and the Chesapeake Bay Bridge-Tunnel, appear. As one drives onto the bridge, the ocean comes close and closer. It is beneath you, then beside you. The expanse of the Atlantic Ocean and the Chesapeake Bay opens before you and as you descend in to the tunnel, you plunge into the great shellfish bay, nature's work of art from fireball to complex ecosystem, and transportation wonder.

*Satellite Image Chesapeake Bay*
*Image Courtesy of Wikimedia Commons*

# A Short Geological History of the Mississippi River

Lock & Dam No. 11, Upper Mississippi River, Dubuque, IA
Photo courtesy of the Library of Congress

*Eventually, all things merge into one, and a river runs through it." - Norman Maclean (American Author 1902-1990)*

The Mississippi River ("Misiziibi": a river spread over a large area to the Algonquin speaking Native Americans) is the largest river system in North America. Its headwaters begin in Lake Itasca, in western Minnesota where the river flows southwards eventually reaching the Gulf of Mexico at the Mississippi River Delta. With tributary headwaters extending from the Appalachians to the Rockies, the river drains all or parts of 31 states. With an overall length of 2,340 miles, the Mississippi River is the fourth largest river in the world. But has it always been this way?

*"There is something fascinating about science. One gets such wholesale returns of conjecture out of such a trifling investment of fact." - Mark Twain, Life on the Mississippi (Mark Twain was a 19th century newspaper writer and author, who in 1863 began to use a pen name derived from a river navigation term meaning two fathoms or 12 feet, a vertical distance with sufficient depth for safe steamboat passage.)*

The Mississippi River's basin originates in Precambrian times (570 Ma[1]) when there was one single continent. At that time, the earth's crust, at the present

---

[1] Ma denotes one million years ago

location of the Mississippi River, was locally stretching, and small rift zones, insufficient to separate the large continent, developed. With further crustal stretching, faults were created within the rift zones, and within these *failed rift zones*, the early Mississippi River valley was borne. As time passed, other continents did form but, by the end of the Pennsylvania Period (290 Ma), previously separated continental masses (tectonic plates) were colliding. With these collisions, the early Appalachian Mountains formed and the landscape was thrust upward in an arching fashion. This arching action led to separation and rapid weathering along the faults within the *failed rift zone* and led to the formation of a distinct proto river valley system that quickly accumulated sediment shed from the Appalachian Mountains.

As time passed, the proto river valley sunk with the weight of accumulated sediment. By the Cretaceous Period (65 Ma), sea level rose more than two hundred feet above present sea level and a large inland bay formed extending from the present Gulf of Mexico to the present confluence of the Ohio and Mississippi Rivers. This bay (also known as the Mississippi Embayment) accumulated sediment at elevated sea levels, and during this time period the embayment became a well defined trough with the rift features plunging with accumulation of sediment load. This embayment retained its basic feature until the more recent Pleistocene Ice Age where at maximum glacial extent (c. 25,000 years ago), sea levels plunged to more than 300 feet below the present sea level, at which time a well defined river valley emerged creating other distinct landforms including scarps and river terraces and creating steepened stream gradients and accompanying rapid erosion of stream beds. With the last glacial retreat (c. 8,000 years ago), sea level rose to approximately its present level and the Mississippi River as we now understand it emerged. Sea levels continue to rise slowly through the present as we now live in an interglacial period. Never the less the Precambrian fault zones, i.e. the *failed rift zones*, are now buried very deeply beneath the Mississippi River, and remain quite active with recurring (weekly) seismic activity. In fact, the 1811-1812 New Madrid Earthquakes (near St. Louis), that are associated with these deeply buried faults, remain the largest earthquakes ever recorded in North America. These quakes even caused the Mississippi River to flow backwards for a brief period of time. As recently as February 21, 2012, there was a magnitude 3.9 earthquake[1] in southeastern Missouri having an epicenter located within the New Madrid Seismic Zone. The earthquake shattered windows and cracked walls locally and was felt in 13 states.

> *"It is strange how little has been written about the Upper Mississippi...there are crowds of odd islands, bluffs, prairies, hills, woods and villages...of course we ignore the finest part of the Mississippi."* - Mark Twain in an interview in the Chicago Tribune, July 9, 1886

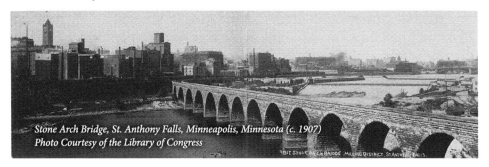

*Stone Arch Bridge, St. Anthony Falls, Minneapolis, Minnesota (c. 1907)*
*Photo Courtesy of the Library of Congress*

The official starting point (or headwaters) of the Mississippi River is Lake Itasca, named by explorer Henry Schoolcraft, in 1832, by combining the last four letters and first three letters of the Latin phrase "veritas caput", which he translated as "true head." From these headwaters to the head of navigation at St. Paul, Minnesota, the Mississippi is a clear fresh stream winding through a country side of lakes and marshes. As the river further descends in this reach, it flows past steep limestone bluffs while it ever so slowly increases in size receiving water from tributaries in Minnesota, Wisconsin, Illinois, and Iowa. The Upper Mississippi is defined by a series of limestone, sandstone and dolostone bluffs that were carved by water from melting glaciers at the end of the last ice age. As the glaciers receded, the racing meltwater stretched from bluff to bluff carving in places the dramatic vertical bluff faces we see along the upper river. This upper Mississippi extends to the mouth of the Missouri River, near St. Louis, where for its first 1,150 miles of descent, it drops approximately 940 feet in elevation from its headwaters. At present this reach of the river makes its descent through

---

[1] The magnitude is a number that characterizes the relative sizw of an earthquake, and is based on measurement of the maximum motion by a seismograph

**121**

43 dams, the largest of which is the site of the St, Anthony Falls in downtown Minneapolis and the location of the only true falls on the Mississippi River.

*"The river is a strong brown god: sullen, untamed and intractable." - T.S. Eliot, American poet and a native of St. Louis, from The Four Quartets.*

*Eads Bridge, St. Louis, MO. - Middle Mississippi, Photo courtesy of the Library of Congress*

Below the Missouri River junction, the middle Mississippi follows a 190-mi course and drops 220 feet in elevation as it reaches the mouth of the Ohio River.

At times the turbulent, and cloudy Missouri River, adds enormous quantities of silt to the otherwise clearer Mississippi. Traveling from north to south, this reach of the river is not dammed and the volume of water is significantly greater due to the contribution of flow from the Missouri River, whose source at 8,000 feet is Brower's Spring which lies along the Continental Divide in southwestern Montana.

The current form of the Mississippi River basin was largely shaped by the retreat of glaciers during the most recent Ice Age. Glacial meltwaters greatly enlarged the trough along the course that the Mississippi River now flows. Additionally, a buried deep layer of material washed out from the ice sheets accumulating to thicknesses of 100 to 300 ft in this middle section.

*"And they talked about how Ohio water didn't like to mix with Mississippi water. Ed said if you take the Mississippi on a rise when the Ohio is low, you'll find a wide band of clear water all the way down the east side of the Mississippi for a hundred mile or more, and the minute you get out a quarter of a mile from shore and pass the line, it is all thick and yaller the rest of the way across." - Mark Twain - Life on the Mississippi (originally written for Adventures of Huckleberry Finn)*

The Lower Mississippi River meanders leisurely and descends 315 feet from its junction with the Ohio River at Cairo, Illinois to then form the lush delta at the edge of the Gulf of Mexico, for a distance of nearly 1,000 miles. From a transcontinental flight, the sunlight glistening on the twisted ribbon of the one and one half mile wide Mississippi River is a distinctive landmark. What is also quite evident when viewed from the air is the myriad of oxbow lakes and cutoffs, testifying to a geologically active river constantly changing and correcting its course over long periods of time. The study of the river's ever changing patterns, falls under the geological term: fluvial geomorphology. As recent as March 1876, a flood moved the river several miles away from a small section of the border of Tennessee and Arkansas. Since this event was an "abandonment", or properly termed an avulsion, the state line remains located in the old (and now abandoned) channel. At present, there are no dams along this reach of the river, however tall levees and bank stabilization efforts have been constructed to create a highly channelized river.

*"The Mississippi River will always have its own way; no engineering skill can persuade it to do otherwise." - Mark Twain in Eruption*

Flood control along the river dates back to the construction of the city of New Orleans in 1717 by the French, who built a small levee to shelter their infant city. While flooding along the river channel is an annual concern and has been the chief agent for change in recent geological history, the year 2012 marks the 85th anniversary of the most devastating flood in recorded history along the Mississippi River. The nation's most destructive flood began with heavy rains in the summer of 1926 which continued throughout the spring of 1927. Three separate flood waves occurred on the lower Mississippi in 1927-in January, February and April, increasing in magnitude each time. In the spring of 1927 many of the levees failed, the worst of which at Mounds Landing, Mississippi, flooding an area 50 miles wide and 100 miles long (the size of the state of Connecticut) with up to 20 feet of water. By July 1, 1927 the waters finally began to recede, but 1.5 million acres of land was still under water, with the disaster leaving behind more than 500 people dead and over 700,000 people displaced from their homes. The catastrophic flood of 1927 fostered a commitment by the federal government to initiate a definite program of flood control by the construction and maintenance of a complex array of riverbank structures rationally designed to contain and divert floods for the entire reach of the lower Mississippi.

*"About fifteen miles above New Orleans the river goes very slowly. It has broadened out there until it is almost a sea and the water is yellow with the mud of half a continent. Where the sun strikes it, it is golden." - Frank Yerby (American Writer)*

Although no glaciers reached the lower Mississippi Delta region, its influences have transformed the surrounding lands and specifically the river Delta. High water flows combined with sediment loads of the glacial melt waters initially created braided stream patterns which developed into existing meandering patterns and the eventual redepositing of sediment load within the river Delta in layers tens of feet in thickness. In addition to the annual deposition of wind blown and fluvial deposits at the mouth of the river, a natural process known delta switching has historically shifted its final course of the river's mouth to the Gulf of Mexico every thousand years or so. This occurs because the deposits of silt and sediment begin to clog its channel, raising the river's level and causing it to eventually find a steeper, more direct route to the Gulf of Mexico. Geologists consider the next major change in the course of the Lower Mississippi is now overdue; flood control structures and other engineering measures holds the mouth in a tentative state of equilibrium.

*Crescent City Connection, New Orleans, LA – Lower Mississippi.*

*"All rivers, even the most dazzling, those that catch the sun in their course, all rivers go down to the ocean and drown. And life awaits man as the sea awaits the river." - Simone Schwarz-Bart (American Author)*

But does the river end at the Gulf of Mexico? NASA MODIS (Moderate-resolution Imaging Spectroradiometer) images clearly indicate that the fresh river water flowing from the Mississippi into the Gulf of Mexico does not mix into the salt water immediately. The images show a large plume of fresh water which stays intact and flows through the Gulf of Mexico, which then flows into the Straits of Florida, and eventually mixes with the waters of the Gulf Stream off the southeastern coast of Georgia.

# Recollections of a Young Construction Engineer on the Verrazano Narrows Bridge

*The year is 1960. A recent graduate of Manhattan College's Civil Engineering program is heading out into the world and his boss says: "Jim, your job for the next year or so is to perform some construction engineering on a somewhat modest construction project – and by the way it's the Verrazano Narrows Bridge."*

*Verrazano Narrows Bridge – Looking North*

Before his passing, the author had a small dialogue with an elderly, eminent engineer, who shared some wistful reflections of some exciting construction times of more than a half century ago.

*Where were you living at that time?*

At that time, I was living at the north end of Manhattan Island overlooking the Harlem River and the Henry Hudson Bridge. After graduation I worked briefly at American Bridge's Ambridge Plant in Pennsylvania; then within a few months I relocated to Trenton, NJ and then very quickly I arrived in New York City.

*What was your involvement with this monumental engineering project?*

My personal involvement with the Verrazano Narrows Bridge project goes back to the early 1960's when I was transferred to the Engineering on Broadway in lower Manhattan. The engineering team I was a part of was responsible for the design and development of the procedures and special equipment used to erect the bridge.

*What years did you work there?*

I spent 10 years of my career in New York City starting in December of 1956 before ultimately returning to Pittsburgh. The New York office of American Bridge, one of several engineering offices throughout the country, was the office where all engineering related to suspension bridges was assigned.

11176           MARCH 1975           CO1

## JOURNAL OF THE CONSTRUCTION DIVISION

### FIFTY-YEAR DEVELOPMENT: CONSTRUCTION OF STEEL SUSPENSION BRIDGES

By James D. Dwyer,[1] M. ASCE

#### INTRODUCTION

A review of the development of the methods used in the construction of suspension bridges over the past 50 yr reveals a progression of changes in the methods used to erect the major elements. The elements affected include the main cables, cable wrapping, towers, and suspended steelwork. These changes will be illustrated by reviewing the erection of several of the major bridges built in the United States during this period. Until recently, the design and construction of long-span suspension bridges has been found primarily in the United States. The majority of these have been built in the period between 1925 and the present. This paper will be limited to it description of parallel wire suspension bridges built in the United States during this period. New design concepts recently used in Europe will be described at the conclusion of the paper.

#### HISTORICAL DEVELOPMENT

The first suspension bridge in the United States was built in Pennsylvania by James Finley in 1796. He was granted a patent for a cable comprised of a chain of hand-forged links. The bridge had a span of 70 ft and was 13 ft wide. In the years immediately following, many suspension bridges were built using this type of cable.

In 1844, John A. Roebling introduced the use of parallel wire in the main cable and, in 1854, on the Niagara Falls Bridge, he introduced the concept of aerial spinning. During the period between 1844 and 1870, Roebling constructed 10 suspension bridges.

The era of the modern suspension bridge may be considered to have begun with the construction of the Brooklyn Bridge. The design of the bridge commenced

Note.—Discussion open until August 1975. To extend the closing date one month, a written request must be filed with the Editor of Technical Publications, ASCE. This paper is part of the copyrighted Journal of the Construction Division, Proceedings of the American Society of Civil Engineers, Vol. 101, No. CO1, March, 1975. Manuscript was submitted for review for possible publication on November 13, 1974.
[1] Engr., American Bridge Div., United States Steel Corp., Pittsburgh, Pa.

105

*Jim Dwyer, then and now (c. 2010)*

*What was the state-of-the-art in construction engineering for suspension bridges at that time?*

This was the golden era for suspension bridge construction for the New York office of American Bridge. In a period of less than 10 years, work was performed on the on the Delaware Memorial, Walt Whitman in Philadelphia, Ogdensburg and Massina over the St. Lawrence Seaway, the Throgs Neck and Verrazano Narrows in New York City, the 25 de Abril

Bridge over the Tagus River and the Angostura Bridge over the Orinoco. I am hankful to have been part of it.

*What technologies were at work at that time?*

The most important single structure handled by the New York Office of American Bridge was the Verrazano Narrows Bridge. Our contract was to furnish, fabricate and erect the four main cables and suspended steelwork. The cables were composed of 61 strands within a diameter of 36 inches. The cables have a total weight of 38,000 tons and are made up of 145,000 miles of 0.196 inch diameter wire. The engineering team was tasked with the design and development of the procedures and special equipment used to erect the cables and suspended steel. This included design and fabrication of the tramway for spinning the cables and the 20-foot-wide catwalks, cable erection calculations, truss units erection and sequencing, computation of suspender "no load" lengths, guide wire calculations and barge stability calculations used in the delivery of the prefabricated truss units.

*What exactly is cable spinning?*

The cable is perhaps the most unique aspect of a suspension bridge. The basic method of cable spinning in 1960 was much the same as it was is 1880. Pairs of spinning wheels shuttle back and forth from both anchorages simultaneously on the same cable, laying down wires parallel to each other in carefully predetermined positions. For the Verrazano Narrow Bridge, we rigged four foot diameter spinning wheels so that each wheel would carry two, not one, loops of wire. It took about 15 minutes for both pairs of wheels to make the trip from one anchorage to another, a distance of 7,200 feet. The cables were laid in a hexagonal pattern of strands that were compacted, banded and wrapped. In a week's time we were able to spin as much as 2,500 tons of cable.

*Can you tell me a few personal highlights?*

At the time of the bridge opening in late 1964, I was overseas. In a phone call my wife told me my 5-year-old daughter told her kindergarten class and teacher that her Daddy had received a medallion for building the Verrazano Narrows Bridge, which was the subject of a school newspaper article that week. A medallion was to be given to people who had worked on the bridge by the Triborough Bridge and Tunnel Authority, the owner of the structure. Being met with some doubt, my daughter wanted to take the medallion, which had just arrived, to school to prove she was right. Needless to say, it did *not* happen and to this day I have the medallion, a certificate and a photo of the bridge in a frame.

*Photo courtesy of Jim Dwyer*

*Were you involved with any publications on this project at that time?*

Not at the time; but…this experience and many others with American Bridge led to a request to prepare and submit a paper on the development of suspension bridge construction techniques for the Journal of Construction Division of the ASCE's 50th Anniversary Issue. It was published in March 1975.

*What were you most lasting memories; what were your greatest impressions?*

I have three very distinct and different memories which have lasted a lifetime. First, believe it or not, the view from a barge with a truss unit in place queuing for erection while the Queen Mary was passing by. She entered the upper bay traveling at a slow rate of speed, in fact almost dead in the water. I still remember her rail crowded with passengers gazing in utter wonder. Second, when chance would have it, and I ascended one of towers, I would take in the view. The view of lower Manhattan from the towers cannot be described. Third, the people I met who were leaders in the profession. These leaders include Milton Brumer, Herb Rothman, Frank Stahl and Jack Kinney, all key members of the design team. These leaders also include my mentors on the American Bridge engineering team; these experienced engineers generously shared their knowledge and passion while training the younger staff in the interesting and complex world of construction engineering.

## Some Historical Notes

The Verrazano Narrows Bridge is named for Florentine explorer Giovanni da Verrazzano, the first known European navigator to enter New York Harbor and the Hudson River, while crossing the Narrows. Fort Lafayette, constructed during the war of 1812 and renamed in 1825, was a coastal fortification in New York Harbor. The fort was demolished as part of the bridge's construction in 1960; the Brooklyn-side bridge tower now occupies the fort's former foundation. The 13,700-foot-long bridge, designed by Amman & Whitney, marks the gateway to New York Harbor. Its center span of 4,260 feet is the longest of any suspension bridge in the United States. The bridge was the last great public works project in New York City overseen by Robert Moses, the New York State Parks Commissioner.

*Verrazano Narrows Bridge over the Hudsone River*
*Photo Courtesy of the Library of Congress*

# CHAPTER 6

# THE VIADUCT

*viaduct* - a long bridge-like structure carrying a road or railroad across a valley or other low ground

*"Thus, from this slight and very short experiment, we may understand and judge of the mighty and wonderful laws of the heavens and the nature of winds."*

*Vitruvius, De architectura (now known as The Ten Books of Architecture), Book 1, Chapter 6, c. 30 BCE*

# ... The Viaduct ...

## ... a Viaduct over a Viaduct ...

*Joe Montana Bridges, Toll 43, Washington County, Pennsylvania*
*Tallest Bridges on the Pennsylvania Turnpike System*
*Photo Courtesy of Gannett Fleming, Inc.*

# Look Up! *(some historic railroad)*
# *Viaducts in the Sky*

*The Starrucca Viaduct, Lanesboro, PA, USA*
*Photo courtesy of the Library of Congress*

The one hundred year era from 1850 to 1950 may be considered the golden era of railroad bridge construction in North America. As a quilt work of railroad lines began to crisscross the continent, an exciting variety of structural forms captured the imagination of the public as magnificent railroad viaducts, imaginative in shape and daring in construction, bisected large valleys and deep, rugged terrain. At first wood, then stone, then briefly iron, quickly followed by steel and concrete superstructures became the major building blocks, and breath taking, high level railroad structures began to silhouette the landscape. The imagination of the engineers and the daring ingenuity of the contractors of this era are captured by the tales of three viaducts in the sky.

## The Starrucca Viaduct

*"... Vedi, Veni, Vinci ..." (Latin) – '... I came, I saw I conquered ...' – Juliius Ceasar, Gallic Wars*

The year is 1848. The main modes of transportation are the horse, wagon, stage coach ... and canal. A new mode of transportation is on the horizon – the railroad. The shareholders of the New York and Erie Railroad Company envisioned a railroad from Lake Erie to the Hudson, just north of New York City. To assure that their charter with the state of New York will not lapse, the planners needed to have the railroad line completed to Bingham, New York, along the Susquehanna River, near the New York/Pennsylvania Border before the year ends. The best alignment included a small stretch of right of way through Pennsylvania – and the last obstacle was the crossing the steep walled valley of the Starrucca Creek, a tributary of the Susquehanna. The plan was audacious – build, as the Romans did centuries before, a stone viaduct based on classical lines and principles.

> " ... I can build the viaduct in time, provided you don't care how much it cost ..." - James P. Kirkwood, engineer in charge of construction

So boasted the construction engineer, assigned by the railroad. (Fortunately, the railroad did not care about costs given the looming deadline.) The year of 1848 saw a frenzy of activity in the Susquehanna River Valley with 800 local laborers engaged in the construction of an engineering feat worthy of a Roman aqueduct. From a seemingly continuous line of wooden falsework, a 17 span, 100 foot tall, 1,040 foot long viaduct quickly emerged. With mules, horses, rail carts and simple derricks, the workers quarried, cut timber and constructed an engineering icon.

For the stone columns and semi-circular stone arches, nearby Pennsylvania Bluestone (a common local term for limestone) was quarried and dressed. Each stone was individually fitted and marked for installation. The most striking feature during construction was the wooden falsework constructed continuously, from span to span ahead of the stone arch construction. Given the constraints of time, the decision was made to fully support the entire structure with falsework, thereby quickening the erections of the masonry. The falsework was removed after the last span was completed.

*Construction Engineering in the Golden Age of Railroad Bridges*

Continuous Wooden Falsework

Starrucca Viaduct — 1848

Rivet Traveler

Erection Traveler

Rivet Platform

Temporary Struts

High Level Bridge at Lethbridge — 1909

300' Tall Wooden Erection Tower

Erection Cable

Delivery Bucket

Umbrella

Umbrella

Tunkhannock Viaduct — 1915

Illustrations are based on historical photographic records and other historical documentation.

Casey Palmer

After one hundred and fifty years of service and only routine maintenance, The Starrucca Viaduct is not only a beautiful structure with striking lines but remains a symbol of our railroad heritage, representing its daring and enterprising spirit at the time of its infancy.

# The Canadian Pacific High Level Bridge at Lethbridge

*"... the noise echoed throughout the river valley, especially on still days, and seemed ... to go on forever ..." (recollections of Oliver Watmough recalling, as a boy from his nearby childhood farm, the noise of the pneumatic riveting hammers driving 328,000 field rivets.)*

The year is 1908. At the eastern edge of the Rocky Mountains in the high plains not far north of the US/Canadian border lies the city of Lethbridge, situated on a high plateau above the nearby Oldman River. In the late summer, word buzzed in the town of the new railroad line that would be built to transport coal from the Rockies and would cross the large river valley immediately to the west of town. The valley, though tranquil, was quite imposing, as the Oldman River meandered in a broad valley lying 300 feet below the wind-swept plateau that the City was founded on.

The summer of 1908 was rather quiet. In the valley floor, trees were being cleared, concrete was being poured, and curiously, an occasional diver was spotted entering the deep waters of concrete caissons at the valley floor. And then the valley walls echoed with the rhythmic percussion sound of steel rivet installation, continuing through the fall, winter, spring and into the early summer days of 1909. At first slowly then with deliberate pace, a large skeletal structure emerged from the high plateau and proceeded westward. At first a span, then a tower; then a span, then a larger tower, cycling onward for over one mile until the entire valley was spanned. Leading the construction was a large steel erection traveler with 85 foot long cantilevered arms hoisting steel in front of it, with the pieces growing bigger and bigger as the valley grew deeper. Behind the large traveler followed a smaller, but not insignificant wooden traveler with suspended cages of workman installing rivets and generating the loud percussion noises heard throughout the valley floor. As the bridge seemingly built itself across the broad river valley, the bridge's unique shape appeared, a rhythmic pattern of short yet deep steel girder spans and slender inclined leg steel towers, silhouette in appearance.

*The High Level Bridge at Lethbridge, Alberta, Canada*

Its design was unique in some respects. To reduce the wind front on trains atop the viaduct, the track was embedded within the walls of the girders, not unlike the conventional deck girder designs of the day. In the days of only a rudimentary knowledge of geotechnical engineering, flooding, consolidation settlements and ground water movements were particularly troublesome for the river foundations and the spans of the western slope. The 1908 flood caused considerable difficulty and delays in the construction of foundations, which otherwise were smoothly preceding the rhythmic march of the towers and superstructure. A particularly troublesome location on the west slope, immediately above the river valley, required the construction of deep vertical and then horizontal entry shafts. These shafts were constructed solely for the purpose of exploring the soils and ground water flow to determine why a particular tower was constantly settling and to eventually develop a plan for a significant hillside buttress and caisson supported underpinning.

*" ... In Lethbridge stands a railway bridge, that holds the wand'ring eye. The highest longest of its kind, our Viaduct in the Sky! - from a poem by Larry Varty, 1999*

On the twenty-third of June, 1909 the last steel span was placed and on the next day, the first train crossed the structure. The completed structure, 5,300 feet in length and 314 feet at its highest point, was in 1909 and remains to the present (2020), the largest railroad bridge of its kind in the world.

## Tunkhannock Viaduct

" ... [it is a] ... thing colossal and impressive ... Those arches! How really beautiful they were. How symmetrically planned! And smaller arches above, how delicate and lightsomely graceful! It is odd to stand in the presence of so great a thing in the making and realize that you are looking at one of the true wonders of the world."
- Theodore Dressler, 1916, Hoosier Holiday, a travel biography.

The year is 1914. War is breaking out in Europe; but to the folks in Nicolson, Pennsylvania, a small community 20 miles north of Scranton, a most impressive concrete structure is taking form. From May of 1912 to December of 1915, this small community's population has soared to support a 500 man work force to build the Delaware, Lackawana and Western (DL&W) Railroad's largest structure – at that time and for the next fifty years, the largest concrete railroad bridge in the world.

In 1912, Abraham Burton Cohen imagined a colossal viaduct, designed on principles established in antiquity and patterned after the Roman aqueducts such as the Pont du Gard – as series of small equally spaced circular arches supported on large, symmetrical circular arches. Cohen's design is impressive – twelve 180 foot symmetrical arches, 2,400 feet of viaduct, 240 feet in the air. Each arch is separated by wide banded concrete columns, giving the structure a distinct and stylistic appearance. But how to build it?

The construction engineering, led by F. L. Wheaton of the DL&W RR, is even more impressive than its design. By the winter of 1912, large excavations were being made into the earth to support the structure. The volumes of concrete cast within the earth equaled the volumes of concrete of the massive and impressive columns, arches and deck visible above ground. Several foundations were particularly troublesome, requiring a pressurized sunken caisson at one location, where a "quick" soil condition required the sinking of the last 20 feet of a 65 foot deep excavation thru the weight of cast concrete above.

The Tunkhannock Viaduct, Nicholson, PA, USA
Photo courtesy of the Library of Congress

By the spring of 1913, three impressive wooden erection towers were constructed along the structure centerline, one lying at the middle of the valley floor and rising to a height of 300 feet, and two others lying 1,500 feet to the north and south. To support a tramway for the delivery of materials, two large cables continuously spanned between the imposing wooden erection towers. Marching symmetrically from the northern and southern slopes, the massive concrete arches began to emerge. As the construction progressed, the columns took form, followed by the construction of the "umbrellas" – so called by the local town folk. But what were the "umbrellas"?

By the early 20th century, construction engineering had progressed to the stage that fabricated structural steel elements, utilizing efficient structural forms were available for temporary construction works. The so-called "umbrellas" were pairs of slender, three - hinged, steel arch, support trusses – where the central (upper) hinge was adjustable by ratchet to allow elevation control for form centering. Multiple pairs of "umbrellas" were pre-fabricated so that more than one arch span could be constructed at any given time. The construction progressed from the valley walls to the center of the valley with the last span cast around the tallest erection tower.

When completed, the visions of Cohen and Wheaton were realized, and another vital link of railway connecting Lake Eire and New York City was completed.

> *"Those of us who live in its shadow often seem to take it for granted, and yet, we are never unaware of its grandeur or might ..." The Bridge was Built, Nicholson Area Library. Currently the bridge is owned by the Canadian Pacific Railway and conveys CP and N&S freight traffic.*

*A Footnote: Besides the Starrucca Viaduct, the High Level Bridge at Lethbridge and the Tunkhannock Viaduct other notable, high level railroad bridges, to name a few, from the golden age of railroad bridges include: two (still extant) nearly 200 foot tall wooden trestles, one on Vancouver Island (Canadian Forest Products Englewood Logging Railway) and one near Skelton, Washington on the Olympic Peninsula (Simpson Logging Railroad); Roebling's Double Decker Niagara Suspension Bridge (no long longer in existence); the 300 foot tall Kinzua Viaduct, sadly partially destroyed by a tornado in July of 2003; The 1910 PL&E cantilever bridge (767 foot main span) over the Ohio River, near the confluence of the Beaver River, the colossal Quebec (cantilever) Bridge over the St. Laurence River in Ontario, Canada (with its 1800 foot main span, reminiscent of the Firth of Forth Bridge in Scotland) ;as well as the Eads Bridge (St. Louis) and the Huey P. Long Bridge New Orleans), both crossing the Mississippi River.*

# Lessons from the Kinzua

*Earth science, engineering, emotions ...* Seldom does one witness a confluence of three such seemingly diverse abstractions which converged in an unrelenting encounter on the afternoon of July 21, 2003. On that day, the pinnacle of early 20th century railroad engineering faced an unusual meteorological event that precipitated the collapse of an engineering icon, the Kinzua Viaduct, a structure, listed on the National Register of Historic Civil Engineering Landmarks and the jewel of the Pennsylvania State Park System. As the principal investigator for the collapse, the author, along with a team of engineers, material specialists and earth scientists, witnessed, first hand, the aftermath of nature's fury and the raw emotion of those who witnessed the collapse. As we sifted through the debris field, the team came to determine not only the engineering mechanics of the disaster but also came to appreciate a new understanding of the nature of wind flows in an extreme meteorological event.

*The Kinzua Viaduct* – an historical setting: With rapid growth in the extraction of mineral resources during the late 19th century, the Commonwealth of Pennsylvania saw the development of a complex railroad transportation network, one that spanned the many gullies, valleys and gorges of the western and north-central parts of the state. Fossil fuels, especially coal, were needed in Great Lakes cities, and rail was the transportation of choice. Within the steep Kinzua gorge the original viaduct was constructed in 1882, a forty-one span structure, constructed principally of iron with its signature, patented wrought iron Phoenix columns. At the time of construction, the 301 foot tall structure was the tallest in the world. With the advent of heavier rail loads in a time of rapidly changing technology, the bridge was dismantled in 1900 and, the structure was rebuilt as a forty-one span structure with identical span and grade line as the first Kinzua Viaduct. With the decline of the mining industry the railroad was eventually sold to the Commonwealth who, in 1970, made the viaduct into the centerpiece of the state park system by permitting both an excursion railroad and visitors to traverse the lofty viaduct and admire the scenery and structure. The author too has been a visitor of the state park and shared many enjoyable moments with his son and his son's friends. Trains rumbled over the Kinzua gorge for more than 100 years, riding rails atop a marvelously slender structure. On the afternoon of July 21, 2003, however, the viaduct's service came to an abrupt end when it was attacked from the strong winds of a tornado, and 23 of its 41 spans collapsed in spectacular fashion.

***Earth science – the meteorological phenomena:*** A series of unfavorable weather conditions produced a severe weather event on July 21, 2003. On that day, an intense weather system, called a mesoscale convective system, formed in the afternoon within a wide area including eastern Ohio, western Pennsylvania, western New York and southern Ontario. The intense system produced a series of spiral like cloud banks, which moved in counter clockwise direction as the entire mesoscale convective system moved in an easterly, northeasterly tracking direction. At the leading edge of the front, the contribution of wind shear and moisture with afternoon instability initiated intense thunderstorms. Tornado activity appeared due to intense smaller vortices within the larger mesoscale convective system. At Kinzua State Park, an F-1 tornado, recognized as a tornado event with wind speeds as high as 112 mph, touched down at approximately 3:20 pm local time. The distinct, large scale, forested debris fields at the site revealed that the structure was attacked in a matter of seconds by two separate and distinct wind flows, differing 90 degrees in orientation. The forensic investigation determined that initially the counterclockwise (cyclonic)

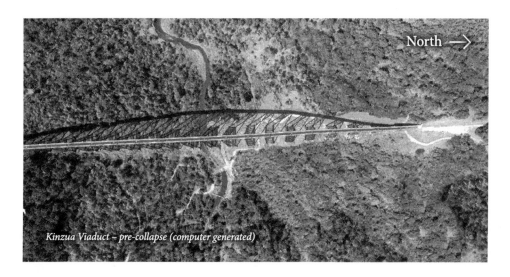

North —→

*Kinzua Viaduct – pre-collapse (computer generated)*

wind within the northward moving vortex attacked the structure sideways with straight line winds from a due easterly direction. Then, as the swirling vortex moved northward, the structure was reattacked by a concentrated flow of southerly straight line winds, an inflow phenomenon that supplied wind energy to the vortex.

***Engineering – the collapse:*** In the course of a forensic investigation, numerous indicators, or *forensic markers*, are identified that, when taken collectively, reveal the secrets of the event.

At the Kinzua site, there were four particularly apparent forensic markers:

- Order markers: which reveal the chain of events identifying the distribution of materials clustered within the debris field.

- Directional markers: which reveal wind direction, based on a broad overview of the direction of fallen trees and collapsed towers.

- Separation markers: which, at the location of "clean"—that is, fresh— "breaks" reveal failure points in materials.

- Fracture markers: which, under magnification, reveal the nature of small-scale fractures within the high stress points of the structure.

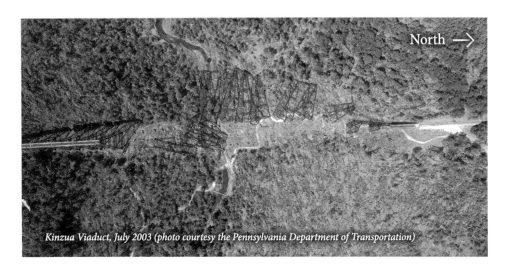
*Kinzua Viaduct, July 2003 (photo courtesy the Pennsylvania Department of Transportation)*

The four forensic markers revealed that the failure was initiated at the location of the connection of the viaduct's elegant superstructure to its substructure. In particular, when the viaduct was reconstructed in 1900, the new superstructure was mounted on the existing foundations and the superstructure was secured to the existing wrought iron anchor bolts of the original construction. The new superstructure was fitted with provisions for lateral expansion which could only be accomplished by extending the anchor bolts on the eastern face with a collar coupling assembly. Over the years, the assembly, hidden from view by a series of washers, developed radial cracking attributable to rusting and thermal actions within the structure. In essence the coupling assemblies could not maintain a tensile load path from the anchor bolts in the substructure to the tower legs in the superstructure, which left the structure vulnerable to uplift, however, only in the event of strong winds from a direction opposite the prevailing wind direction. With wind forces sufficient to produce uplift on the easterly foundations and no internal system redundancy, the towers supporting the superstructure collapsed progressively from the south to the north. The forensic investigation concluded with precaution, that much of our aging infrastructure, such as tower viaduct systems, may be "wind susceptible" with potential for "weak-link" details hidden from ordinary view.

*Wind debris field; note tower collapse in two directions indicating separate wind directions in a single meteorological event.*

***Emotions – eyewitness encounters and personal reflections:*** The emotions are best expressed by individuals in their own words.

*"It was raining and blowing very hard as I left the trailer and I hear a series of boom, boom, booms, like thunder … Leaves and branches were starting to fly so we hurried to our truck …" [and unable to leave the park due to downed trees they returned to the bridge site and then] "… It looked all right at first, but when we got closer, we saw that the whole middle [of the bridge] was gone. Then I realized the booms I'd heard were the towers hitting the ground one by one …"* – *the pensive words of Floyd Quillin, the on-site construction supervisor, whose keen recollections were crucial in the course of the investigation, as his attestation confirmed the analytical work of the forensic investigators.*

*Kinzua Viaduct Observation Platform (2011)*

***Epilogue:*** Kinzua State Park has reinvented itself after the 2003 disaster. Even though the debris field remains as it did in the late afternoon of July 21, 2003, even though trains no longer traverse the viaduct and even though one can no longer walk its length and survey the wondrous landscape of the Allegheny Mountains and the gorge, one can walk a small portion of the viaduct length to a viewing platform built upon one of the remaining standing towers, survey the debris field and pause to give wonder to power of nature. The park visitors can also view the nearby interpretive center, which describes in relevant terms the results the forensic investigation's findings. And the engineer and layman alike, who now view the site, can begin to develop an appreciation for the raw mixture of ***earth science, engineering and emotions*** that converged on a hot and humid July afternoon.

# Kinzua Memories

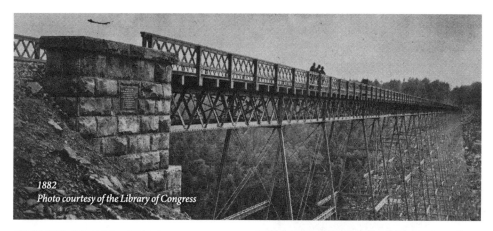

1882
Photo courtesy of the Library of Congress

Original Viaduct (1882)
Photo courtesy of the Library of Congress

Rebuilt Viaduct (1901)
Photo courtesy of the Library of Congress

On July 21, 2003, a 301-foot-tall railroad structure spanning a gorge in north-central Pennsylvania collapsed dramatically as a tornado touched down just east of the structure. A bridge that was the tallest in the world, when built in 1882, and that had carried trains for more than a century after it was rebuilt in 1900, was gone in just 30 seconds. Twenty-three of the viaducts forty-one spans catastrophically collapsed. The forensic investigation conducted in 2003 for Department of Conservation and Natural Resources determined that steel elements connecting the towers to the foundations at the east tower bases had fractured, making the structure, with its south to north orientation, vulnerable from winds from the east, which would only occur in the cyclonic flow of tornado winds.

Relive the history of the magnificent structure, which was an integral part of Kinzua Bridge State Park, the jewel of the Pennsylvania State Park system, through the eyes and expression of many who were truly close to the bridge. These eyewitness accounts, from both professional and lay perspectives, emote strong feelings of accomplishment, fear and wonder.

*"We'll build you a bridge a thousand feet tall...if you'll provide the money"*

Aldolphius Bonzano, Phoenixville Bridge Company to General Kane owner of the New York, Lake Erie and Western Railroad and Coal Company Railroad deciding between two alternative routes to the north; one was the construction of four miles of tortuous, twisting two percent grade; the other the erection of a railroad viaduct loftier than any yet built by men. The General had the money and built the first Kinzua Viaduct in 1882. The Phoenixville Bridge Works assembled the Kinzua Viaduct in an amazing 94 days.

*"..as the Great Great Grand Daughter of General Kane I have a special spot in my heart for Kinzua Bridge and the whole Allegheny Forest Area...I have traveled with my husband and daughters there several times and am always in awe in the majesty and beauty of the area and the bridge"* :

Susan Sclafani, Largo, FL, Family Descendant of General Kane, builder of first Kinzua Viaduct, as reported in Find Yourself in the Forest, Allegheny National Forest Vacation Bureau www.visitanf.com

*"To span the valley, the Kinzua Viaduct had to be the loftiest Structure of its kind on earth. "*

W. George Thornton, Erie Railroad Magazine, August 1949. The structure was rebuilt in 1900 to handle heavier trains. The rebuilt viaduct maintained the same grade line, the same foundations and same spans as the original viaduct. The company's chief engineer, Octave Chanute (the same Octave Chanute whose glider research would later inspire the Wright brothers) was instrumental in both the design of the first and second Kinzua Viaduct. Trains rumbled over the gorge until 1959 when it was sold for scrap.

> The Kinzua Viaduct is a "truly heroic nineteenth-century railroad bridge…it has stood rusting in a remote part of northwestern Pennsylvania ever since the Erie Railroad abandoned it in 1959, but its future is far happier than that of most unused bridges."

David Plowden, Invention and Technology Magazine, Winter 2003. Nick Kovalchick, a scrap and salvage dealer, got the contract to demolish the viaduct, but he could not bring himself to destroy such a beautiful structure, and he persuaded the state to build a park around it. Kinzua Bridge State Park and sold the bridge to the state in 1970 for the exact amount of money he had purchased the bridge from the Erie Railroad Company.

> "A picture I have kept on my desk through three hard years of architecture school is my youngest brother and two eight year-old friends playing at the Kinzua Viaduct on a clear June day in 1998. …I measure nearly every building I visit against that moment with my brother at the girders of the viaduct. As I visit architectural landmarks, I ask questions of them, not of my architectural education, but of the childhood railroad bridge where I climbed as though life stood still. Would Wright's Falling Water invite children to play on its foundation? Would the Pompidou Center spark Paris tourists to race as they climbed its long staircase from bottom to top? Would parents and their babies at Gehry's Bilbao gleam with pleasure as they touched its curving metal walls?"

Rebecca Shaffer, Eugene, Oregon reported in *Find Yourself in the Forest*, Allegheny National Forest Vacation Bureau www.visitanf.com In 1977, the Kinzua Viaduct received national recognition when it was placed on the National Register of Historic Civil Engineering Landmarks.

*"To everything there is a season ... a time to be born, ... a time to ... "*

Ecclesiastes 3. On July 21, 2003, a series of unfavorable weather conditions produced a mesoscale convective system accompanied by intense storm fronts, encompassing eastern Ohio, western Pennsylvania, western New York and southern Ontario.

Numbers denote failed tower numbers

*"... all hell broke loose ... trees were falling all around ... the wind was howling like I have never seen or heard before..."*

Shawn Baker, construction worker and eyewitness to the July 21, 2003 collapse. The weather system produced a series of spiral-like cloud banks that moved in counterclockwise direction as the mesoscale convective system tracked in an easterly direction. At the leading edge of the front, the combination of wind shear and moisture within afternoon instability initiated intense thunderstorms and a series of tornadoes along the Pennsylvania/New York border.

*"It was raining and blowing very hard as I left the trailer and I heard a series of boom, boom, booms, like thunder. Leaves and branches were starting to fly, so we hurried to our truck, and by the time we reached the park gate, the trees on either side of the road were bending down toward each other... it took us a while to climb through the downed trees and wreckage to a point where we could see. It looked all*

*right at first, but when we got closer, we saw that the whole middle was gone. Then I realized the booms I'd heard were the towers hitting the ground one by one."*

Floyd Quillin, Site Construction Superintendent, W. M. Bodie Co., July 21, 2003, reported by Katie Jaeger, *Invention and Technology Magazine*, Winter 2004. The tornado produced a complex damage pattern, most likely the results of its fast forward movement and its interaction with the rugged terrain. The structure was attacked by easterly leading edge winds due to the cyclonic motion of the tornado and from the south by inflow winds generated by the tornado. In some locations tress were blown in multiple directions.

*"[it] just laid over on its side."*

Barrett Clark, manager of Kinzua Bridge State Park, who came to the site to find trees snapped off, a tangle of debris, and after freeing a park worker trapped inside a collapsed shed viewed the bridge. Pittsburgh Post Gazette, Wednesday, July 23, 2003

*"After 121 years, viaduct falls victim to tornado." - Pittsburgh Post Gazette, Wednesday, July 23, 2003*

*"As professional engineers, we often design and build structures, such as the Kinzua Viaduct, albeit seldom of its magnitude. However, rarely does the opportunity arise to step outside the purely quantitative realm of design codes and material properties to conduct an investigation in the manner of a detective or private investigator."*

Jonathan McHugh, a member of the team of engineers and scientists which conducted the (Board of Inquiry) forensic investigation of the collapse for the PA DCNR, *PE Reporter* March/April 2006.

*"When a magnificent structure like this falls down, it drives home the importance of documentation ... Though this is certainly not the ending we had anticipated, we are going to follow this story wherever it leads us... This tornado is just one more event in the life of the bridge."*

Lisa Gensheimer, video documentarian, reported by Katie Jaeger, *Invention and Technology Magazine*, Winter 2004

*Failed "Collar Coupling" assembly*

*The failure initiated at the base of the towers. Several "Collar Coupling" assemblies, connecting the base of the 1900 construction to the 1882 construction, experienced "cracking", a considerable time before the collapse. The cracking was not visible by inspection as the washers (rear of photograph) "covered" each assembly.*

*With the stong easterly winds and cracked "collar coupling" assemblies, the bridge towers separared form their foundations during the wind event of July 21, 2003.*

*"We ran the tourists until October of 2004, but for the two years after the bridge closed, the number of riders declined by 75 percent,"*

Teri West, daughter of owner of The Knox & Kane Railroad which opened in the early 1980s and started carrying passengers over the 301-foot high, nearly half-mile long bridge in 1987, prior to the sale of entire inventory from steam engines to lanterns, reported in The Daily Item, September 28, 2008.

> *"I've had people from Vermont, West Virginia, Maryland and even Vancouver, Canada, contact me about some of the items in the auction."*

Mike Peterson, whose auction and realty company in Jamestown, N.Y. ran the sale of the Knox & Kane Railroad, reported in The Daily Item, September 28, 2008. Not to be dissuaded, the owner of the structure, Pennsylvania Department of Conservation and Natural Resources, developed bold plans to strengthen the portions of the damaged viaduct and maintain the site as an interpretative center, attesting to the power of nature.

> *"It would be an octagon out at the end with a see-through floor…If you go all the way out to the end of what's left, it's about a 220, 240-foot drop."*

Jason Zimmerman, manager of the park complex, describing ambitious plans of the Pennsylvania Department of Conservation and Natural Resources to restore the site as an interpretive center which would include construction of a see-through platform on one of the remaining towers, as reported by Dan Majors, Pittsburgh Post-Gazette, March 2, 2009.

*New viewing platform, completed in 2011.*

# CHAPTER 7

# LOOKING BACK AT HISTORY

*history* - the study of past events, in human affairs

*"If you would have your wish come true, the covered bridge you must go through." - Margaret Wister Meigs (Preservation Advocate), 1941*

# Looking Back at History

*King's (Covered) Bridge*
*Over Laurel Hill Creek*
*Somerset County*
*Pennsylvania*
*Constructed 1806*
*Restored 2008*

*Joggle joint, mortise and tendon, lap splice, ogee washer, tree-nail pin, trunnel pin and dowel pin – a few of the unique vocabulary terms associated with the covered bridge - while common terms in the 1800s, they have moved into oblivion in our modern lexicon.*

*The American Timber Covered Bridge is often assumed to have risen from American Soil. As early as 1735, information on such bridges became available in Germany. America took the idea of the covered bridge with alacrity. The earliest covered bridge in America was constructed across the Schuylkill River in Pennsylvania in 1806.*

*The largest number of Covered bridges in the United States, totaling more than 200, are located in Pennsylvania.*

*Photo is courtesy of Gannett Fleming, Inc.*

# *The Romance of the Covered Bridge*

*" ... my little horse must think it queer, to stop without a farmhouse near ..." Robert Frost, Stopping by Woods on a Snowy Evening*

Who has not paused to look at and reflect upon a covered bridge? What motivates us to drive many miles out of our way and look at these disappearing symbols of rustic Americana? In 2013, a contest was held to collect the best photographs of covered bridges in America. Enjoy the best of the best. Hear what the judges of the contest had to say. And ... reminisce in the words of a poet.

*Crossing over the covered bridge*
*hearing the click click as we go*
*over each and every piece of wood*

*Haverhill Bath Covered Bridge over the Ammonoosuc River, Woodsville, New Hampshire*

*Judges Comments: "... a beautiful bridge in a most interesting natural setting ... a great reflection of the ingenuity of its builders ..."*

**155**

*Looking out and seeing the river below*
*how the snowcaps from the evergreen*
*seem to wrap its edge with warmth*

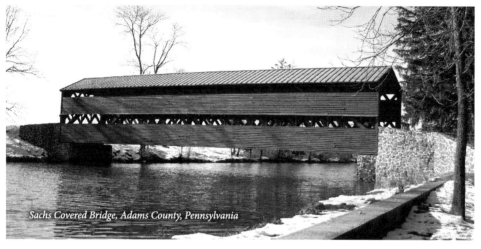

Sachs Covered Bridge, Adams County, Pennsylvania

*Judges Comments: " ... intriguing symmetry ... a handsome form ... in a crisp winter setting ..."*

*So many times as a child we would go*
*over this covered bridge, and never*
*really understanding, how we were intruding*
*on mother nature's serenity*

Tohickon Aqueduct (Delaware Canal National Landmark), Point Pleasant, Pennsylvania

*Judges Comments: " ... a beautiful bridge setting ... a creative photo composition ..."*

*Flying off in a scuff, a very angry hawk*
*either got its pray, or was about to leach*
*down for its kill*

Ashuelot Covered Bridge, Winchester, New Hampshire

*Judges Comments: " … creative geometric context . .. fascinating perspective …"*

*Memories still stay in my mind of that old*
*road, with the river's edge so pleasant to view*
*in summer and a winter's wonderland in the cold*

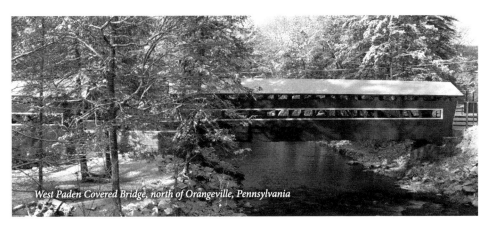

West Paden Covered Bridge, north of Orangeville, Pennsylvania

*Judges Comments: " … pleasant winter composition … with a hint of a twin nearby …"*

*Today the bridge is gone, the area now has*
*been purchased, and all that remains is*
*just a vacant view, as the trees were all cut,*
*and mother nature was robbed again*

*Union Covered Bridge (over the Elk Fork of the Salt River), Monroe County, Missouri*

*Judges Comments: " … a beautiful twilight composition with an interesting color contrast …"*

*Forever in my mind I will hold the scenery*
*in my heart, as the distant cries of various*
*birds a chatter, and the squirrels scattering*
*up the rivers bank's fallen acorns*

*Corbin Covered Bridge over the Croydon branch of the Sugar River, northwest of Newport, New Hampshire*

*Judges Comments: " … a tranquil mood with contrasting colors and reflection …"*

*The same sun rises and falls each day*
*however never will it shine as it did*
*when the old covered bridge was there .....*

*Flume Covered Bridge, Lincoln, New Hampshire*

*Judges Comments: " ... stopped by woods on a snowy evening ..."*

*Poetry passages from The Old Covered Bridge A poem by Bonnie Collins, Contemporary Poet*

# If Bridges Could Talk

The bridges of New England are charming … but … what if they could talk? What story would they have to tell? Listen!

My name is the Stanwich Road Bridge. I am located in Greenwich, Connecticut. I was constructed in 1937. I am one of the many rigid frame bridges crossing the Merritt Parkway. The distinctly unique architectural elements of me and my sister bridges were conceived by George L. Dunkelberger of the Connecticut Highways Department. These architectural elements which included experimental forming techniques were inspired by the Art Deco and Art Moderne styles of the 1930s.

Photos are courtesy of the Library of Congress

My name is the Main Street Bridge. I span the Israels River, a small tributary of the Connecticut River, in Lancaster, New Hampshire. I am one of 40, but the last remaining extant two span, cast in place, reinforced concrete spandrel, multi-rib arch bridge designed by the Daniel B. Lutton in the state. I was constructed in 1929. I am the sixth bridge at this location, preceded by two wooden bridges, one covered bridge, and two iron bridges. Natural disasters, mostly flooding, caused the destruction of my predecessors.

*Photo is courtesy of the Library of Congress*

My name is the Eagle Lake Bridge. I am a part of the Acadia National Park Road System and am located in Bar Harbor, Maine. My Gothic (pointed arch) features are only one of two such bridges within the National Park. I am the most visible of the 18 stone faced bridges built by John D. Rockefeller to restrict automobiles from using his carriage road system. I was designed by William Welles Bosworth, a graduate of the Ecole des Beaux Arts in Paris, France. I was

*Photo is courtesy of the Library of Congress*

built in 1927 and am now viewed by more park visitors than any other bridge in the park.

*Photo is courtesy of the Library of Congress*

My name is the Taftsvile Bridge. I am located in Windsor Vermont. I was constructed in 1838. I am a two span bridge, 189 feet long, supported by a modified king post truss, supported by a semi-independent arch. I am not a patented bridge type but am a survivor of early craftsman tradition, possibly influenced by Swiss tradition at the time of my construction. My builder was Solomon Emmons III.

*Photo is courtesy of the Library of Congress*

My name is the Mianus River Bridge. I was built in 1904, I am located in Greenwich Connecticut and I am a rolling lift moveable bridge. I, as well as eight other lift bridges on the system, carry AMTRACK, along the Northeast Railroad Corridor in Connecticut. Originally I was a part of the New York, New Haven and Hartford Railroad (commonly known as the New Haven - NH), which was a railroad that operated in the northeast United States from 1872 to 1968 and served the states of Connecticut, New York, Rhode Island, and Massachusetts. The NH's primary connections included Boston and New York City.

Photo is courtesy of the Library of Congress

I am the Charles River Bridge. I carry the MBTA Commuter Rail traffic from the northern Boston Massachusetts suburbs across the Charles River into North Station (Fleet Center – Boston Garden). I am one of four double track, single leaf, rolling-lift, bascule bridges that were built in 1931, replacing the former steam driven, jackknife and swing bridge predecessors. Sadly only two of us remain. My span is approximately 90 feet in length and my counterweight weighs 629 tons. My lift mechanism is powered by an electric motor.

Photo is courtesy of the Library of Congress

I am the Court Street Bridge. Named in 1896 after the construction of the nearby court house, I span the Blackstone River in Woonsocket, Rhode Island. I was built in 1895 and am a Pratt Truss with pinned connections and stamped eyebars for diagonals and lower chord members, a rare example of a 19th century steel deck truss. As a Pratt Truss, all of my diagonals are subjected to tensile forces only. In many ways I am structurally deficient due to aging and deterioration and I will be eventually replaced.

*Photo is courtesy of the Library of Congress*

I am the Buzzards Bay Bridge over the Cape Cod Canal and am considered considered the railroader's "Gateway to Cape Cod". On the morning of December 29, 1935, a passenger train from Boston to Hyannis was the first train to cross me. I was constructed by the Public Works Administration and I am the second bridge constructed at the site. Since 1935 my iconic silhouette, with signature towers and elevated truss span, has dominated the horizon of the south shore of Cape Cod as well as the open water of the Atlantic Ocean. I carry railroad traffic (mostly waste and some excursion traffic) across the Cape Cod Canal, connecting Cape Cod with the rest of Massachusetts. While most lift bridges are kept down for land traffic to cross and lifted to allow boat traffic to pass under, I am one of only a few lift bridges in the United States kept in an up position and only lowered for the occasional land traffic.

At the time of construction, with a 544 foot main span, elevated 136 feet above high tide, I was the largest vertical lift bridge in the Country.

I remain a silhouette icon. Perhaps you have traveled to Cape Cod and have seen me in person. But how well do you know me? Take this short 10 question quiz;

test your knowledge of American history, biology, railroad engineering, civil engineering and electrical engineering.

*Q1.* The first vertical lift bridges in the US were designed by Squire Whipple; these lift bridges predate the construction of the Buzzards Bay Bridge. – T or F

*Q2.* The buzzards after which Buzzards Bay is named are not really buzzards at all but osprey. – T or F

*Q3.* In 1623 Miles Standish of the Plymouth Colony and other Pilgrims dug a small canal in the low lying land between the Manomet and the Scusset Rivers, thus connecting the Atlantic Ocean between the north and south shores of the cape, forming the first Cape Cod Canal. – T or F

*Q4.* The original purpose of the railroad was to ferry passengers to the cape; this still remains the main source of revenue for the railroad. – T or F

*Q5.* The counterweight in each tower, weighs approximately 1,000 tons. Each counterweight provides a factor of safety against uplift of approximately one and one half times the weight of the superstructure. – T or F

*Q6.* It only takes four 150 horsepower motors to lift the entire bridge. – T or F

*Q7.* The bridge's foundations rest on oak piles. - T or F

*Q8.* As the counterweights, to some extent, balance the load of the superstructure, there is in fact very little weight bearing on the foundations. – T or F

*Q9.* Once the bridge is raised and locked in the fully raised position, bridge control sounds three short blasts, three long blasts and three short blasts of the bridge's horn, to signal marine traffic that the bridge is fully raised. – T or F

*Q10.* The Buzzards Bay Bridge remains the longest lift span bridge in the United States. – T or F

---

*A1.* T – In 1872, Squire Whipple, one of the pioneers of American Bridge Building, began to design and build short lift spans with small rises to cross the canals of New York State.

*A2.* T – Yes. An osprey, sometimes known as the sea hawk, is a large raptor, a fish-eating birder of prey 24 inches in length with a 72 inch wingspan. It is brown on the upperparts and predominantly greyish on the head and underparts, with a black eye patch and wings.

*A3.* F – The idea of constructing such a canal was first considered by Miles Standish of the Plymouth Colony in 1623, but this effort failed. Many other attempts made through the 19th century either ran out of money or were overwhelmed by the project's size. On June 22, 1909, construction finally began for a working canal, albeit beset with many problems, including excavation of mammoth boulders left behind by the retreat of Ice Age glaciers.

*A4.* F – The bridge is used today mostly to haul trash to an incinerator in Rochester, Massachusetts, on the south shore and for occasional dinner train rides.

*A5.* F –There is no safety factor involved. The counterweights are carefully sized to approximately equal the dead weight of the lift span to facilitate lift with least effort. In fact, the counterweights are actually sized slightly less than the dead weight of the superstructure (or else the superstructure would never seat).

*A6.* T - The lift span is raised and lowered by four 150 horsepower electric motors. It takes about two and a half minutes to fully lower and seat the span. The power is sufficient to overcome the slight negative load imbalance plus an additional allowance for snow load on the structure.

*A7.* T – The bridge is supported by hundreds of driven oak piles.

*A8.* F – In fact there is considerable weight bearing on the foundations, including the weight of the superstructure, towers and counterweights (which approximately equal the weight of the superstructure).

A9 F - Once locked in the fully raised position, bridge control sounds one blast of the bridge's horn, to signal marine traffic that the bridge is fully raised. (Three short blasts, three long blasts and three short blasts is international code for SOS.)

A10 F - The Arthur Kill Railroad Lift Bridge, Staten Island, New York, at span of 559 feet and constructed in 1958, is the longest vertical lift bridge in the United States.

# Some Timeless Memories of Construction

No photos are more timeless than construction photos of an iconic bridge at its seemingly most interesting and sometimes most challenging instant of construction – can anything be more dramatic?

*Photo is courtesy of the Library of Congress*

*Brooklyn Bridge (spanning the East River) New York City, New York, US, c. 1880*

*Photo is courtesy of the Library of Congress*

*Golden Gate Bridge (spanning the entrance to San Francisco Bay) San Francisco, California, US, c. 1933*

*Hell Gate Bridge (spanning the East River) New York, New York, US*

*Eads Bridge (spanning the Mississippi River) St. Louis, Missouri, US, c. 1874*

*Manhattan Bridge (spanning the East River) New York, New York, US, c. 1909*

*Firth Bridge, (spanning the Firth River) west of Edinburgh, Scotland, UK, c.1890*

**169**

# Quotes for the Ages ...

*An assembly of ten of the greatest engineering quotes from antiquity to the present*

The (ideal) engineer should be  ..." a man of letters, a skilled draftsman, a mathematician, familiar with historical studies, a diligent student of philosophy, acquainted with music, not ignorant of medicine, learned in the responses of jurists, familiar with astronomy and astronomical calculations."

> *Marcus Vitruvius, c. 30 BCE, Roman Army Engineer; his written masterpiece, De architectura (The Ten Books on Architecture), dedicated to the emperor Augustus, is the only surviving major book on engineering (architecture) from classical antiquity.*

"I am an advocate for weatherboarding and roofing...not withstanding I am determined to give my opinion as it appears to be right.  It is sincerely my opinion that the Schuylkill Bridge will last 30 and perhaps 40 years   if well covered.  I think it would be sporting with property, to suffer this beautiful piece of architecture...which has been built with expense and danger, to fall to ruin in ten to twelve years."

> *Timothy Palmer, 1806 upon completion of the "Permanent Bridge", a wooden arch railroad bridge spanning the Schuykill River, in Philadelphia, PA.*

## *"...please..."*

*Edward Manning Bigelow, 1889, "father of Pittsburgh's parks" [to Mary Schenley who he persuaded, via a race across the Atlantic in advance of opportunistic land developers, to donate 300 acres of land for a major city park – the bridge on this page is the signature bridge element within this park (Schenley Park).]*

I ..." decree that the San Francisco Bay be bridged immediately."

*Norton I, (celebrated citizen of San Francisco and self proclaimed) Emperor of North America and Protector of Mexico, 1872. [The San Francisco-Oakland Bay Bridge was opened to traffic on Nov. 12, 1936.]*

"Strauss will never build his bridge; no one can bridge the Golden Gate because of insurmountable difficulties which are apparent to all who give thought to the idea."

*Golden Gate Bridge, San Fancisco, CA*
*Photo Courtesy of the Library of Congress*

*Conventional wisdom, c. 1930 [The Golden Gate Bridge was opened May 27, 1937, one year before Joseph Baerman Strauss' death.]*

"Today, bridge building is truly a science; only three decades back it was hardly worthy to be termed an art; while seventy five years ago, in our own country at least, it was no better than a trade."

*J. A. L. Waddell, 1916 [introductory chapter of his two volume treatise on "Bridge Engineering" dedicated to the Emperor of Japan.]*

"We will build you a bridge a thousand feet high …

… if you'll provide the money."

*Adolphus Bonzano, 1881 (to Thomas Kane contemplating the design of the 301' tall Kinzua Viaduct, tallest structure in the world at that time.) The iron viaduct, when completed in 1882 vibrated so intensely with the passage of trains that it was replaced in less than 20 years with a more rigid steel structure.*

*2nd Kiinzua Viaduct, Mt. Jewitt, PA (1901-2003)*
*Photo Courtesy of the Library of Congress*

I … "agree [with critics of my design] with regard to [reuse of] the old [wrought iron] anchor bolts… strong[er] bolts should have been used with superior details…"

*C.R. Grimm, 1901, designer of the second Kinzua Viaduct (ASCE Transactions). [ The Second Kinzua Viaduct catastrophically collapsed on July 21, 2003 during a tornado. Investigators determined that the collapse was a result of a hidden cracking within the anchor bolt system.]*

"It is refreshing to read something not buried in a mass of intricate calculations that are known only to the author."

*E.K. Morris, 1932, Member of the Water & Power Resources Board of PA, Pittsburgh, PA [ASCE Transactions].*

*Cantilever Erection of the Huey P. Long Bridge over Mississippi River c. 1935*
*Jefferson Parish, LA - (designer: Ralph Modjeski)*
*first bridge built across the Mississippi River in Louisiana*
*(Bridge was significantly widened in 2013)*
*Photo Courtesy of the Library of Congress*

"If Ralph Modjeski had chosen a career in music instead of engineering, the world might have gained a famous concert-pianist but would have lost one of its finest bridge designers."

*William Shank, 1966 [Historical Bridges of PA]*

# End Notes, References & Credits

Cover Photographs are Courtesy of Elan Mizrahi Photography.

### Chapter 1 – To Build a Bridge

*Vitruvius: De architectura: The Project Gutenberg EBook of Ten Books on Architecture*, Release Date: December 31, 2006 [EBook #20239] http://www.gutenberg.org/files/20239/20239-h/20239-h.htm#Page_3

Leech, T., Connors, R., "How Far Would You Go To Build A Bridge", *Pittsburgh Engineer* (Special International Bridge Conference Edition), Engineers' Society of Western Pennsylvania, Summer 2020.

Hawley, H., "Schenley Park Bridge over Panther Hollow", *Historic American Engineering Record – HAER No. PA-489*, Library of Congress, 1998.

Leech, T., and Skocik, A. "The Bridges of the National Road - Our Nation's First Toll Road." *Pittsburgh Engineer* (Special International Bridge Conference Edition), Engineers' Society of Western Pennsylvania, Summer 2004.

Kemp, E., Fluty, B. *The Wheeling Suspension Bridge, A Pictorial Heritage*, Pictorial Hisotries Publishing Co., Inc., Charlestown, West Virginia, 1999.

Leech, T., Horas, G., Patton, J. "What Does It Take to Build a Bridge", *Pittsburgh Engineer* (Special International Bridge Conference Edition), Engineers' Society of Western Pennsylvania, Summer 2019.

Leech, T., "The Power of the Triangle and the Tarentum Bridge", *Tarentum Borough Magazine - Crossroads of the Allegheny Valley*, November 2019.

Photograph of Fallingwater, Mill Run, PA is courtesy of the author.

Photographs of the Toll 43 Bridges are courtesy of Gannett Fleming, Inc. During their design and construction, the author served as structure design manager for these spans as a consultant to the Pennsylvania Turnpike Commission.

Photographs of the Tarentum Bridge are provided courtesy of *Tarentum Borough Magazine - Crossroads of the Allegheny Valley*.

Uncredited photos along the National Road (U.S. 40) are courtesy of the author.

All uncredited photographs and images otherwise are provided courtesy of the *Engineers' Society of Western Pennsylvania*.

### Chapter 2 – Art & Architecture

The photographs of the Salginatobel Bridge (as well as the Millau Viaduct in Chapter 2, and the Seine River Bridges in Chapters 2 and 3) were taken during a 2010 field trip of European Bridge Experience sponsored by the Pennsylvania State University for students in the Department of Civil Engineering Technology, Harrisburg, Pennsylvania. The author was the technical liaison for this student experience.

Leech, T., "The Poem and the Bridge." *Pittsburgh Engineer* (Special International Bridge Conference Edition), Engineers' Society of Western Pennsylvania, Summer 2013.

Longfellow, Henry Wadsworth, *The Belfry of Bruges and Other Poems, initially published December 23, 1845,* https://www.bartleby.com/356/39.html, accessed December 31, 2019.

*Cambridge Bridge Commission Report – Construction of the Cambridge Bridge,* 1909, http://openlibrary.org/books/OL7015322M/Report_of_the_Cambridge_bridge_commission_and_report_of_the_chief_engineer_upon_the_construction_of_ , accessed December 30, 2019

Leech, T, "A Leisurely Walk along the Seine River, Fifteen Beautiful Bridges of Paris … Engineering, Architecture & Arts." *Pittsburgh Engineer* (Special International Bridge Conference Edition), Engineers' Society of Western Pennsylvania, Summer 2011.

Leech, T., "The Bridges of the Merritt Parkway." *Pittsburgh Engineer* (Special International Bridge Conference Edition), Engineers' Society of Western Pennsylvania, Summer 2013.

Leech, T., and McHugh, J., "Viaducts of the Mon/Fayette Expressway - Harmony and Height." *IBC 01, The International Bridge Conference Magazine 2001* (Special Article on Bridge Aesthetics), Engineers' Society of Western Pennsylvania, April 2001.

Photographs of the Western Pennsylvania Viaducts are courtesy of Gannett Fleming, Inc. The author served as the principal designer for these spans.

All uncredited photographs and images otherwise are provided courtesy of the *Engineers' Society of Western Pennsylvania.*

### Chapter 3 – The Cable

Leech, T., Horas, G., Patton, J. "Harmonious Rhythm – Bridges with Cables", Pittsburgh Engineer (Special International Bridge Conference Edition), Engineers' Society of Western Pennsylvania, Summer 2018.

Leech, T., "In the Shadow of the Brooklyn Bridge – David Steinman", *Pittsburgh Engineer* (Special International Bridge Conference Edition), Engineers' Society of Western Pennsylvania, Summer 2018.

Steinman, David B., *A Practical Treatise on Suspension Bridges* (2nd edition), John Wiley & Sons, New York (USA), 1929.

Steinman, David B., *I Built A Bridge, And Other Poems*, The Davidson Press, New York, 1955.

"Bridge Quiz", *Pittsburgh Engineer* (Special International Bridge Conference Edition), Engineers' Society of Western Pennsylvania, Summer 2018.

All uncredited photographs and images otherwise are provided courtesy of the *Engineers' Society of Western Pennsylvania.*

### Chapter 4 – The Arch

Leech, T., Horas, G., Patton, J. "The Arch – at the Intersection of Mathematics and Beauty" *Pittsburgh Engineer* (Special International Bridge Conference Edition), Engineers' Society of Western Pennsylvania, Summer 2017.

"Bridge Quiz", *Pittsburgh Engineer* (Special International Bridge Conference Edition), Engineers' Society of Western Pennsylvania, Summer 2017.

"6th Annual IBC Photo Contest", *Pittsburgh Engineer* (Special International Bridge Conference Edition), Engineers' Society of Western Pennsylvania, Summer 2017.

Leech, T., Kaplan, L. "Arch Bridges and Pittsburgh's Greatest Bridge Decade." *Pittsburgh Engineer* (Special International Bridge Conference Edition), Engineers' Society of Western Pennsylvania, Summer 2017.

All uncredited photographs and images otherwise are provided courtesy of the *Engineers' Society of Western Pennsylvania*.

## Chapter 5

Leech, T., "Perfection and Beauty Unsurpassable - the Eads Bridge." *Pittsburgh Engineer* (Special International Bridge Conference Edition), Engineers' Society of Western Pennsylvania, Summer 2012.

Dwyer, J., (Leech, T.), "The Eads Bridge and the Pittsburgh Connection", *Pittsburgh Engineer* (Special International Bridge Conference Edition), Engineers' Society of Western Pennsylvania, Summer 2012.

Leech, T., Kaplan, L. "The Intersecting Legacies of Roebling and Cooper and the Allegheny River Crossing." *Pittsburgh Engineer* (Special International Bridge Conference Edition), Engineers' Society of Western Pennsylvania, Summer 2019.

Leech, T.G. "Bridges of the Chesapeake: the Rhythm of the Tides." *Pittsburgh Engineer* (Special International Bridge Conference Edition), Engineers' Society of Western Pennsylvania, Summer 2010.

Leech, T., "A Short Geological History of the Mississippi River." *Pittsburgh Engineer* (Special International Bridge Conference Edition), Engineers' Society of Western Pennsylvania, Summer 2012.

(Dwyer, J., Leech, T.) "Recollections of a Young Construction Engineer on the Verrazano Narrows Bridge", *Pittsburgh Engineer* (Special International Bridge Conference Edition), Engineers' Society of Western Pennsylvania, Summer 2010. The author interviewed Jim Dwyer, a noted bridge, transit and railroad engineer in 2010; Jim reflected on the state of bridge construction engineering, 50 years in the past.

All uncredited photographs and images otherwise are provided courtesy of the *Engineers' Society of Western Pennsylvania*.

## Chapter 6

Leech, T., "Look Up! (some historic railroad) Viaducts in the Sky" *Pittsburgh Engineer* (Special International Bridge Conference Edition), Engineers' Society of Western Pennsylvania, Summer 2015.

Leech, T., *Reflections of the greatest bridge engineers and architects of the 20th and 21st Centuries*, Essay 21, Word Association Publishers, Tarentum, Pennsylvania, 2017. (Essay No. 21, "Lessons From the Kinzua" is reprinted courtesy of Word Association Publishers.)

Leech, T., "Kinzua Memories." *Pittsburgh Engineer* (Special International Bridge Conference Edition), Engineers' Society of Western Pennsylvania, Summer 2009.

Leech, T., "The Collapse of the Kinzua Viaduct." *American Scientist*, Volume 93, 2005.

Leech, T., McHugh, J., and DiCarlantonio. G., "Lessons from the Kinzua." *Civil Engineering Magazine*, Volume 75, No. 11, November 2005

Leech, T., Ricker II, R., Eppley, J., and Comoss, E., "Anatomy of a Collapse - the July 21st Collapse of the Kinzua Viaduct." *International Bridge Conference Proceedings, IBC-04-61*, 2004.

Leech, T.., et al. "Board of Inquiry Investigation, Report on the July 21st Collapse of the Kinzua Viaduct, McKean County, PA." Pennsylvania Department of Conservation and Natural Resources, December 2003 (full report including an animation of the collapse is available at www.dcnr.state.pa.us).

The author was the Principal Investigator for the Board of Inquiry Investigation of Collapse of the Kinzua Viaduct.

All uncredited photographs and images otherwise are provided courtesy of the *Engineers' Society of Western Pennsylvania*.

## Chapter 7

Margaret Wister Meigs, Preservation Advocate: *The Untold Story*, https://scholarsphere.psu.edu/concern/generic_works/5x633dz88h, accessed January 4, 2020.

Peaslee, J.T., S.H. Petro, and T.G. Leech. "Restoration of the 19th Century King's Covered Bridge." *International Bridge Conference Proceedings, IBC-08-88*, Pittsburgh, PA, 2008.

"IBC Photo Contest – Covered Bridges – 20 Most Beautiful Bridges" *Pittsburgh Engineer* (Special International Bridge Conference Edition), Engineers' Society of Western Pennsylvania, Summer 2013.

Bonnie Collins (Poem Hunter); *The Old Covered Bridge*, https://www.poemhunter.com/poem/the-old-covered-bridge/ (2009) accessed December 30, 2019

All photographs of covered bridges, unless noted otherwise, are provided courtesy of the *Engineers' Society of Western Pennsylvania*.

"Bridge Quiz: Can You Identify the Bridges of New England?", *Pittsburgh Engineer* (Special International Bridge Conference Edition), Engineers' Society of Western Pennsylvania, Summer 2013.

"True or False, How Well Do You Know the Buzzards Bay Bridge?", *Pittsburgh Engineer* (Special International Bridge Conference Edition), Engineers' Society of Western Pennsylvania, Summer 2010.

"Bridge Quiz, Can you name the bridge?", *Pittsburgh Engineer* (Special International Bridge Conference Edition), Engineers' Society of Western Pennsylvania, Summer 2019.

Leech, T., "Quotes for the Ages." *Pittsburgh Engineer* (Special International Bridge Conference Edition), Engineers' Society of Western Pennsylvania, Summer 2008.

All uncredited photographs and images otherwise are provided courtesy of the *Engineers' Society of Western Pennsylvania*.

# ABOUT THE AUTHOR

## *Thomas Leech*

Thomas Leech is the (retired) Chief Engineer, Bridges and Structures, for Gannett Fleming, Inc., Instructor of Civil Engineering at Carnegie Mellon University, a part of the continuing education faculty of the Pennsylvania State University, and author. While employed at Gannett Fleming, he designed bridges, tunnels and highways and conducted forensic studies prior to his retirement. He has published over 50 articles in national and international journals, conference proceedings and magazines. He was a contributing author to the *Cities of the World* - Geology of Pittsburgh, 2015; technical editor of *Engineering Pittsburgh*, ASCE Pittsburgh Section 100th Anniversary Publication, 2018; editor and author of *Reflections ... of the greatest bridge engineers and architects of the 20th and 21st Centuries*, Word Association Publishers (second printing), 2017; and the co-author of *Bridges ... Pittsburgh at the Point ... A Journey Through History*, Word Association Publishers, 2016.

WA